Self-Empl

Financial Independence Through Affiliate Marketing and Passive Income

By K. Connors

PART 1:

AFFILIATE MARKETING

A BEGINNERS GUIDE TO CRUSHING IT WITH COMMISSIONS

By K. Connors

Table of Contents

INTRODUCTION

Affiliate marketing is where you advertise and promote a company's product or service. When a customer follows your link (containing your affiliate ID) to the company and makes a purchase or uses a service, you receive a commission from that company. Commissions can run anywhere from 20-80%! That means if someone is selling a $50 product with a 50% commission you would receive $25 for every sale you send there. If you sold 10 a week you would be making $1000 a month with as little as a few hours of work a week! With the correct affiliate strategy, a campaign like this is easily obtainable and will stay automated after it's initially set up.

Affiliate marketing is when you find a buyer for a product that someone else sells. But why should you find customers for other businesses? Because they pay you every time they make a sale through one of the people you sent to them. This is the "explanation" of what affiliate marketing is, but the concept might not be 100% clear in your mind. That is why I want you to look at this example: Many phone companies have affiliate programs. I don't want to promote any kind of Phone Company, so I'm just going to make up a fake telephone company name: Surracall.

So, Surracall likes to get more customers (because more customers mean more money). What do they do to get more customers? They advertise, right. They have segments on TV, radio, and they put ads in magazines. Maybe they even have a sales team that goes out to companies and people's houses and talks to them - either by phone or in person and tries to get them to switch to Surracall. But Surracall has some clever marketing people on board. And they say: all this is good, but how about some free advertising?

Now what they do is they offer the opportunity to (basically everybody) to sell Surracall phone contracts for them. Let's say that you bring a new customer to Surracell who signs up for a 12-month contract; Surracall will pay you $30. If you bring two new customers, Surracall will pay you $60; if you bring 10 they will pay you $300 and so on. Some people are bringing lots of new customers to Surracall every single day.

So what is Affiliate Marketing?

CHAPTER ONE

WHAT IS AFFILIATE MARKETING?

Affiliate marketing is a mutually beneficial business partnership between a merchant and a website publisher/owner whereby an affiliate is compensated (commission per sale) for every visitor or client provided through his/her effort. In other words, Affiliate marketing is simple and a quick way to offer products and services without creating them yourself.

"By introducing your customers to products or services from other companies or individuals and get a commission on any sales is Affiliate Marketing." Affiliate marketing is not an easy task for the marketers to market the affiliate products successfully. But it's also not as difficult as most of the affiliate marketers typically earn well over six figures a month. The most important for every marketer is to build trust and relationship with the audience and consistently invest the time and effort.

While traffic sources are a significant factor in affiliate marketing success, the relevancy of the traffic is applied to all digital marketing and sales personnel. The key traffic sources can be SEO, social networks, blogging, email marketing, etc. Digital products pay higher commissions than physical products as it requires the least investment and effort to produce and distribute them. You can offer digital downloads to your readers like eBooks, audio/video files, software's, etc., without any additional overhead cost of production or distribution. You can also provide online, hosted and professional services for your local audiences.

HISTORY OF AFFILIATE MARKET

Affiliates need to pay attention; your affiliate network's actions could get you in some serious trouble. If you think that as an affiliate you can just put any advertisement up, regardless of what it's advertising, regardless of the claims, you are seriously wrong. Affiliate Networks already have a history of throwing their affiliates under the bus when it comes to lawsuits and blaming "rogue affiliates." If you are making money from affiliate marketing, you need to examine whether your network is going to cause you financial harm or send you to jail.

The legal standard is generally that publications are not liable for the bad behavior of their advertisers. The courts have been pretty clear about this and have ruled time and time again that the very act of publishing an advertisement does not make the publisher, for example, a newspaper or website, a partner in the advertisements. The only service that the publisher is providing is the actual "space" for the advertisement to be shown. However, for a publisher to assert this independence, the publisher must be completely separate from the advertiser regarding the claims and content of the advertising. The publisher must be only selling "space" for the advertiser, not involved with any other decisions what so ever. Once a publisher gets more involved "there is a potential for greater liability. The greater role one takes the greater risk they take."

In here comes the problem for many affiliates: since they are not supplying just space but work as "partners" with the affiliate networks and the advertiser, they could be held liable for the content of those advertisements. Depending on their involvement with the advertiser, this means that there is a very real possibility that if the advertiser and the network were named in a civil or criminal action, the affiliate could also be part of that action.

It is the difference between being passive and being an active participant in the process. Once you get involved in the decision making of what the advertisement says you open yourself up to liability.

If you are an affiliate, you need to examine the affiliate networks that you work with. If you have been concerned in the past with who pays, you need to look at the partnership you are creating.

Some questions that you need to ask of the networks you work with, plus do your own research.

1. Has the affiliate network ever been the subject of a government action? This is a sure way to know if the company has some issues legally. While government action doesn't mean the company is necessarily a bad player, affiliates need to examine why the actions took place. If they are multiple allegations over time from different entities, be very wary of the company. What is going on inside that company that makes them the target over and over again?

2. Have they been the subject of lawsuits alleging deceptive or other illegal practices? Lawsuits against affiliate networks aren't that common actually. Only a few affiliate networks in the last ten years have been involved with civil actions alleging illegal or deceptive practices, so if you are working with one of those companies you need to wonder what they are doing wrong. These actions usually are against companies that like to play on "both sides of the line" meaning that they want to push the boundaries, depending on good attorneys to protect them.

If you are named in their lawsuit alongside of them, are they going to defend you, pay for your attorney? Most likely they will hang you out to dry.

3. Is the owner a convicted felon or served time in jail for anything over parking tickets? Examine the person behind the company, is this someone you'd let your kids (if you are that old, or have any) hang out with? If they are sleeze bags that you'd be scared to let in your neighborhood, that's probably a good sign. Yes, the industry has several convicted felons owning affiliate networks and worse, registered sex offenders. You need to examine a person's ethics in regards to other people. Do you want to really trust some guy who was caught robbing old ladies of their social security money with your business?

Whatever you decide, realize that your decisions of what affiliate network you work with could affect you in the future. If that affiliate network gets in trouble, don't be surprised, especially if run by a scumbag, that you will find yourself also in trouble.

CHAPTER TWO

HOW TO PUT IT ON AUTOPILOT

To become an autopilot millionaire, you need to establish one or more streams of passive income. You need to have systems in place that are earning positive cash flow for you perpetually on a regular basis, without you having to physically participate actively in the business. Aside from the time, effort, and money to engage in the initial procurement of your system or your investment vehicle, you would not have to do anything further except to check in on it periodically and make any minor modifications, enhancements, or perform any maintenance as necessary.

Other than that, you are free to walk away from it and tend to other things, and you will still be making money, perhaps even while you sleep. Investment vehicles such as stocks, mutual funds, and real estate can turn you into an autopilot millionaire. However, these require a significant amount of money to be put in, in order to generate profit. As the saying goes, "it takes money to make money". But what if you don't have the money to invest? Can you still become an autopilot millionaire? Yes. Absolutely. The Internet is one of the easiest and least risky means to amass your fortune. For example, for an investment of $10, you can make $1,000 in just a few short hours. Thousands of people are already doing it today. Or, if money is still an issue for you, you can do things such as setting up a free website, a free blog, engage in affiliate marketing and make hundreds or thousands of dollars every week. Thousands of people are already earning their living on the Internet.

Many people start out with their Internet business in their spare time, while maintaining their day job. But after some time, their Internet business income begins to exceed their day-job income, and hence they have achieved financial independence. The Internet levels the playing field in this manner because it is a low-risk endeavor. If you make any mistakes, it is easy to pick up the pieces and try again. When it comes to making money on the Internet, it does not always take money to make money.

You might have seen Autopilot Website System and are not quite sure if it's good or bad. Well, it is one of the best money making programs on the net today. Not only does it deliver, but the creator himself helps you on a daily basis.

LOW TICKET vs. HIGH TICKET ITEMS

High ticket marketing usually involves the setting up of a product funnel wherein you offer customers a low priced product to get them to join you and then eventually move them through the funnel to your high ticket products. This is done in order to build trust and relationship. High ticket products can help you earn a long-term income and get you customers for life. If you want to learn more, here are 3 steps to follow.

1. Private label rights: The first question that comes to mind is where to get the low priced products. You can develop them yourself but then you will have to spend more time in developing those products which you can better spend on marketing your high ticket items. Therefore, a good way is to source some PLR

content. You will get access to e-books, audio series and many other private label products at a cheap rate. The best part about PLR products is that you can use them as your own. Now you can start offering these products either for free or for a small price to get prospects to try out your company.

2. Affiliate products: Another great option for developing your product funnel is affiliate products. Browse through Clickbank and discover products which you can add to your funnel. Promote those products to your list and when someone buys them, you earn a commission. Choose products which are reliable because your reputation depends on which products you offer to your list. You can then at the right time, offer your high ticket products and make your bucks. Now that seems like a lot of work but the good news is that you can automate the whole thing and let it run.

3. Auto-responder: This is a tool to help automate your complete list building, sales funnel and conversion process. You will need to plan in advance and design sharp email messages designed to attract audiences to take a look at your offering. Once they sign up for your list, you can keep promoting your PLR content and affiliate products, again through scheduled email messages. Using this you can set it, start it and forget it and you will keep earning money through complete autopilot.

High ticket products require a great deal of planning and foresight. You also need to set up many systems In order to keep attracting the target audience and moving them through the funnel. The above 3 steps are meant to give you an overall idea on how to get started with your high ticket marketing.

CHAPTER THREE

HOW TO FIND PROFITABLE AFFILIATE NICHES

We're going to take a close look at how to pinpoint the most profitable niches. Affiliate marketing starts and ends with finding the right niche to market in. It's pretty simple, really. You find a hotbed of buying activity and you plant yourself firmly there to market as many hot products as possible to a very active market of potential customers.

It's worked for hundreds of marketers who have become very, very rich. But, let's face it - when you're getting started, nothing is ever quite that easy.

So, I want to delve deeper into the idea of niche research, along with the mistakes that so many of us tend to make over and over again. Because, when you can eliminate those mistakes, life gets much easier and the profits are more consistent.

The niche research no-no's

First up, let's take a closer look at what so many starting affiliate marketers do wrong. I've heard, the vast majority (pretty much all people), make their profits almost entirely from one or two niches.

Yes, that's right, it's exactly as it sounds. They spend hours a day working on just dog training, or just marriage advice or just weight loss. They find a profitable audience and they hit them up over and over again with different products, sites, and selling points.

Second, as you might have guessed, they stuck to the big niches - the evergreen ones that have always been solid money makers. Sure, they experiment a little bit, but only enough to check out other niches, not so much that they dilute their income from big one or two niches. Which niches are considered the "big niches"?

Weight loss, making money, satellite TV on PC, muscle gain, self-help, anti-spyware, forex, and money online. People are always looking for new products in these niches, so you cannot cannibalize your sales, nor can you run out of warm leads. Of those niches, weight loss and fitness are the biggest across the board, with making money coming in at a close second.

FINDING A PROFITABLE NICHE

Regardless of what type of online business you are trying to develop, it's a good idea to focus on one specific niche. But picking out a profitable niche online can sometimes be like trying to find a needle in a haystack. The internet is a busy place and online business owners need to know that they are entering a worthwhile market before spending time, money and resources on building up a new internet based business.

FINDING YOUR NICHES AND PRODUCTS

Of course, just saying "try out the stuff that works" isn't very helpful, so I want to go into a bit more detail on what you can promote and how to make your selection. In terms of finding product ideas, do stick to click bank and Amazon and on occasion, use Google to review possible affiliate networks in greater depth.

1. Amazon.com research

Let's start with Amazon.com. I start here because I want to first find a niche that has a large buying base. You can always find a product in Clickbank with high gravity, but even before that, I want to identify the breadth of a potential audience first. You'll see why very shortly.

To start, visit Amazon.com and start reviewing products and topics in niches that you are interested in. This is very important because you'll be spending a lot of your time investing in that niche, especially if it becomes one of your big two niches. So, be sure it's something you're willing to write about and market extensively for months to come. If you could care less about weight loss or are afraid of dogs, those might not be the best paths to success. With that in mind, start searching on Amazon for books, products, and other niche products. Your goal here is to find products with at least 20 reviews. Why just 20 reviews?

Considering the fact that Amazon estimates only 1 in 1000 people actually review something they buy from their site, a product with 20 reviews is likely to have been purchased by at least 20,000 people - that's a huge market, especially if it's just one product in an information niche.

If you can find multiple products in the same niche that all have 20+ niches, you've hit the jackpot. It doesn't matter if the niche has 100 products or just 2; if there are people buying products, it's a good niche.

You don't need to do any keyword searching, competitor research, or product searches, because you know you've found a good one.

2. Moving to click bank

With that in mind, it's time to find a product that you can actually market. In general, I don't recommend promoting physical products on Amazon. With only a 5% commission (to start), you'd only make $1 on a $20 book, and most Amazon products are on massive reductions, so profit potential is limited for info products.

If you find a highly valuable product in a niche like 'solar energy kits' or 'home stereo equipment', you might rethink that, because you can make $15+ per sale. Generally speaking though, you should never choose a niche where your minimum commission per sale is less than $15. That should be your magic number. So, with that magic number in mind, we take a stroll over to ClickBank - the number one affiliate network on the Internet, where info products are sold by marketers like you and me for commissions up to 75%. A single $20 book on ClickBank will get you a profit of between $10-$15 - much better for the time you invest into it.

11

For most popular info niches (the major niches we discussed at the beginning you'll find dozens of products. I recommend sticking to these major niches because they have more options and have proven conversion rates. Seasonal and specialty niches require more work and are hard to focus on in the long term.

Look for a $ per sale of at least $15. Ideally, you'll get even more than this - upwards of $30+ per sale. Additionally, look for a gravity of at least 30. The gravity represents how many affiliates have successfully sold that product in the last few weeks. The higher the number, the better it converts and the more room there is in the market for you to join in. Later, you'll need to review the competitor sites to be sure you can find a place for your own websites, but for now, just identifying the niche is enough.

3. Heading to Google

Of course, ClickBank is not the only affiliate marketplace and if you find a product on Amazon that doesn't show up in Clickbank, you still have other options. Go to Google and search for "niche affiliate program".

Many times, other networks will pop up with plenty of options. A big chance for profit here would be in CPA networks that offer non-info product opportunities with massive chances for profit.

GETTING IT RIGHT

There is no right answer for which niche you choose to work in. But, if you're even remotely serious about being successful and becoming the next big super affiliate, you need to pinpoint a rich, evergreen niche that can be solicited time and again for profits without boring you to tears. Do that, and you're well on your way to a successful marketing plan.

With that marketing plan in mind, it will be time to start building sites and funneling traffic into your new affiliate marketing empire.

TIPS ON HOW TO FIND A PROFITABLE NICHE ONLINE

1. Google suggests. When you type a word into Google before you hit enter it displays a list of possible phrases that you may be looking for. This auto-complete feature draws on popular search requests from other users. Because an audience are searching for that item it is likely to be a profitable online niche.

2. Amazon. When you're looking for a profitable niche online business Amazon has already done a lot of the work for you. If a niche market is popular among the world's largest retailer that will quickly tell you if you have a workable marketplace or not.

3. Magazines and Books. You can also use the offline world to search for a profitable niche online. The publishers of magazines and books do a lot of research before spending money on marketing and printing, so when you see a book or magazine for sale, it's most likely based on a top niche market.

4. FAQFox.com. FAQFox.com scans online forums and scrapes keywords and phrases based on a word that you enter. It will list titles, links, and questions that are relevant to your keyword. When you see a lot of people talking about the same problem, product or service that shows there is a profitable niche online.

5. Udemy.com. This website shows markets where people are buying courses and education. You can use their information database to see a list of the most popular courses. This is a great way to find out what people are actually paying money for.

6. Ask technorati. You can search for your niche subject matter on this website. If there are a good number of results, you are probably a profitable online niche.

7. The competition. If there are lots of businesses in a market that is very competitive, it will be challenging for you to be successful. However, if there is no competition it shows that it is not a viable market. Type your niche name into Google. If there are ads related to the search that's a good sign. That means companies are profitable enough to spend money on advertising in your market. Now you need to focus your efforts on a well-defined segment of that market.

CHAPTER FOUR

WATCH OUT FOR SCAMS

Well, if you are reading this chapter, then you probably have heard of Wealthy Affiliate and are scouring the internet to find that post, equivalent that tells you that Wealthy Affiliate is a scam. I bet you haven't found it yet either, have you? Well, that's because the short answer is no, Wealthy Affiliate is not a scam.

You have to stay on top of what's going on with the internet, your advertisers, different search engines, etc. Keeping up to date with the best ways to generate traffic is a must and research, research, research.

Sound tough? Well, it definitely can be. But that's why Wealthy Affiliate is such a great resource. There are a bunch of tools that you gain access to with Wealthy Affiliate that can cost tons of money elsewhere; and once you get the hang of what you are doing, you find that you start using just about all of them! And probably the best resource at Wealthy Affiliate is the forum. There are a bunch of people that post in the forum to answer questions and help people along. And I'm talking about people that are doing this for a living so these guys know what they are talking about. And here's a little piece of advice about the forum. If you see one of the guys who are obviously doing well at internet marketing post some advice...you'd better write it down. These guys know what they are talking about and if they give you a secret, you definitely want to follow up on it!

Well, that's about the gist of it. It is no get-rich-quick scheme and will take some doing, but once you learn it, you may just find yourself working from home making more money than you thought possible on the internet and enjoying life a whole lot more!

SEO STRATEGIES

Everyone wants to attract more eyeballs on their website. Sound and effective search engine optimization (SEO) strategies have the potential of getting your site to the top of Google's organic search rankings, leading to the growth for your business. SEO is a fast-moving field. Hence, it is no surprise that you will find people getting swept up in new advancements, trends, and practices. However, there are some gold standards in SEO that all affiliate marketers should adopt.

1. Define your audience. SEO drives traffic. But that would be of no use if your products is not showing up in front of a relevant audience. Hence, it is in fitness of things that you should identify the type of audience you are targeting and know their search patterns, demographics, geographic location, preferences, etc. A step in this direction can be made by setting up a Google Analytics account that will enable you to learn more about them on a daily, weekly, monthly basis.

2. Put your audience first. When creating your posts, it's an absolute must that you have a buyer-first mentality. What your buyers were really getting out of the writings should be uppermost in your minds.

3. Never assume you have no direct competitors. There will be always someone who has already used the keywords you wish to target. Do your homework to find out who these competitors of yours are and how you can differentiate your SEO strategy from those of others.

4. Improve your page speed. Google lays great emphasis on page speed. A great page speed improves the visibility of your site. Research shows a second delay in a page's load time can decrease the customer dissatisfaction by 16 percent. This is all the more important in the case of mobile users.

5. Use long tail keywords. Using long long-tail keywords in your strategy is key to the success of your business. For instance, considering the keyword "SEO tips" may take a long time for improving the ranking on Google. However, using long tail versions of the keyword "SEO tips" such as "SEO marketing for your business" can increase your chances of raking high on Google.

6. Local SEO. Small businesses need to be especially focused on local search. If you are a small brick-to-brick business, local SEO is of utmost importance. It has been found recently that 50% of those consumers searching locally on their smartphone visit a store that same day. The figure stands at 34% when it comes to search on a computer or tablet. Hence it is in fitness of things that your business's visibility should rank high in your area. Otherwise, you run the risk of losing out to competitors.

7. Get your website compatible for mobile devices. Findings of a survey reveal that 60% of traffic is coming from mobile devices and that number is likely to increase. Hence it is incumbent on you to ensure that your site is optimized for mobile visitors and not difficult to navigate on mobile devices.

This becomes all the more necessary because Google is in the process of awarding higher ranks to the sites that are mobile optimized.

8. Voice search. With the passage of time, the use of voice-based search is increasing. It is now clear that you can ignore voice search at your own peril. Since voice search queries differ greatly from typed queries, you will have to optimize your content for voice search.

9. Be authentic. SEO is not a sneaky or deceptive practice, even though there are people who tend to think so. Tricking search engines by using shady tactics is not going to help you. By doing so you run the risk of losing the trust of search engines.

10. Focus on quality over quantity of links. Quality rather than quantity should be your prime consideration when it comes to building your affiliate links. Cranking out mass number of links without quality has the potential of damaging your website's credibility.

HOW TO GET ORGANIC TRAFFIC?

There are many guides out there today that will claim to make you rich without doing any work or putting in any effort.

Whenever you are trying to get traffic for a new product or website your first thought should be trying to get organic traffic because it "organically" (freely) advertises your products without the need to exert additional effort once it is established. If you can establish long-term brand recognition or traffic flow then you will be guaranteed to make money and it will also be from a "passive" source as you do not need to exert any additional effort to make money off the products for which you are an affiliate.

To get organic traffic; the first is finding a product that will actually convert visitors into paying customers.

The second is actually converting these visitors into some kind of profit using affiliate products and proper landing pages.

The third part is "Unleash a Wave of Traffic..." which is all about finding targeted organic traffic for your products and sites.

The fourth part is a new form of SEO that hasn't been tapped yet, allowing you to rank highly in a short period of times in major search engines such as Google.

The fifth part actually is to know how to create your own products and then start your own affiliate programs so that others will make money for you.

The sixth and final portion is for you to know how to replicate your results so that you will not be dependent on a single stream of income that rests at the mercy of search engines.

CHAPTER FIVE

OUTSOURCING

Outsourcing is becoming a common development among specific industries and services. Outsourcing can be defined as subcontracting a service to a third party company to provide a service that could otherwise be performed by in-house workers. Simply put, outsourcing refers to a transfer of a business function or a service to an external, third-party service provider.

Many large-scale and medium scale businesses are getting more and more involved in outsourcing as the years go by. An example of jobs being outsourced are call centers that run services such as technical support, credit cards, medical transcription, and even bill payments. These third-party companies either handle different jobs or they do offer the same service but cater to a wide range of clients. Most of these jobs are situated overseas or offshore and are usually located in developing countries.

Only recently has outsourcing been used for a lot of specialized services but outsourcing itself has been around for a long while. Specific specialized services like company payrolls, billing and data entry are outsourced in order to have these services done more efficiently. Specializing in a specific process does not only make the service more efficient, it also makes it more cost-effective. Lower operational costs and specialized services are some of the main reasons why foreign companies resort to outsourcing.

Companies have a lot of reasons to outsource their services to other countries but one main reason why they do that is because they save a lot of time and money which is perhaps the most important aspect of it all. One of the reasons why companies want to outsource to developing countries is because the payroll and the benefits are not as expensive compared to the mother location.

For example; the minimum wage of an employee in the Philippines is nowhere near the minimum wage that an employee in the United States has to be paid. Benefits such as health care, bonuses, wages cost much lower if you outsource to developing countries than availing them at the business' original location.

Information technology outsourcing and business process outsourcing are perhaps the two most popular types out of the several forms of outsourcing. Outsourced information technology services often mean the transfer of computer and internet related labor.

On the other hand, business process outsourcing involves call center outsourcing, human resources outsourcing, investment and accounting outsourcing, and claims processing outsourcing. IBM and Accenture are just some of the biggest companies that are involved in business process outsourcing. Outsourcing also has its disadvantages like many other business models. One of the disadvantages is the severance of direct ties between the company and their client. Services like customer care are one of the highest priorities in outsourced services nowadays. Another drawback of outsourcing is the loss of jobs in the developed nations because jobs and opportunities are disappearing abroad.

Why is outsourcing necessary?

One of the most prominent reasons companies outsource is to access expertise, experience, and expensive analytical equipment not available in-house. By outsourcing, you can save a great deal of money which will allow you to provide your product/service at a cheaper price and thus increasing your sales and productivity. By outsourcing the company reduces the need to invest capital funds in noncore functions, making capital funds more available for core functions. It can eliminate the need to show returns on equity from capital investments in non-core areas thereby improving certain financial ratios.

Outsourcing allows the company to focus on its greater value adding activities while support services are assumed by an outside provider. It can enable an organization to accelerate its growth and success through expanded investment in areas offering the greatest competitive advantage. It helps the companies become more profitable and leads to better service levels than internal departments can provide.

Whether you need to implement traditional or fully integrated, multi-channel e-commerce strategies, outsourcing solutions deliver the proven, scalable and secure infrastructure you need - from order and information management to billing, website design and hosting, customer service, international distribution services and reverse logistics. It helps to build a customized solution designed to meet the specific needs of your business case. And ensure that it remains dynamic and flexible enough to respond to an evolving marketplace.

Outsourcing is a management tool for redefining and re-engineering the organization. It challenges companies to think beyond the vertically integrated organization in favor of a more flexible organization structured around core competencies and long-term outside relationships.

Web outsourcing company often need to keep skills, certifications, and efforts up to date in order to stay competitive. This effort can become an asset and resource for their clients. Management of technical staff and projects becomes the responsibility of the outsourcing firm, so your company can concentrate on its own business.

CHAPTER SIX

HOW TO CREATE ENGAGING CONTENT FOR CONTENT MARKETING

Content marketing is about creating engaging, useful and value-adding content to the readers, often forming the foundation for a strong digital marketing project.

Content is increasingly important as Google and other search engines are placing heavy greater emphasis on value-adding their users, as well as on-site user experience. These are easily traceable and measurable from Google's range of software, from Google Analytics to Google webmaster tool. We have talked about how having a good Search Engine Optimisation (SEO) can help you in your digital marketing campaign, as well as go through the step-by-step process on how to improve SEO.

How does content marketing fit into digital marketing?

Content marketing is used to sustain the readers' attention through many different ways. One easy use could be to improve the number of page views per visitor in Google. Another could be to increase the average time your visitors stay on site. Another one could be to decrease the bounce rates.

Content marketing is not only done on your website - it could be used with email marketing, social media marketing, advertising, press releases and many more other channels.

Content marketing Agencies is the future foundation of all of your online marketing strategies.

What do you need to create a good content?

Through many projects and experimentations, we found that a good content should aim to achieve the following pointers:

• The content needs to be engaging

• The content has to be credible

• The content should be authoritative

• The content should be educational and teaches something to the readers

Engaging

First of all, a genuine successful content marketing is one that disarms readers of their first encounter and engages the readers on a one-to-one basis. Good content should directly be relevant to your targeted consumers.

One way is to write in a conversational form as readers prefer to read a book that addresses directly to them.

1. Credible

Content must be credible as it directly addresses the company's image.

Effectively using this strategy helps a company become a trusted and reliable source for the readers and potential clients.

2. Authoritative

Showing more authoritative as compared to other competitors in the same field or specialization will give your business an edge over them. There will be more trust build between you and your potential consumers naturally.

3. Educational

The main focus of marketing content is to build the company's branding, not to advertise your products. Ultimately, a good content is to provide values and educational purposes - a new perspective, insightful information.

When we talk about educational content, it should be content that will value-add the readers' lives, be it helping them know more about how your products can ease the problems they face in their lives or just purely information that can benefit them. Don't forget to make your content share-worthy to their family and friends.

How to create engaging content for my content marketing strategy?

How do we start? Here is an easy template which you can immediately use for your own content marketing strategy:

First, we can identify keywords with the potential to let us reach out to our potential clients and readers.

We can also write content about solving a problem that your potential customers and readers face. Lastly, we can talk about a current event and news

What are the various resources we can tap on to create engaging content?

Google Trends

One of the ways is Google trends, which we can start as a research tool. You can find out what keywords are in your niche right now and what keywords are on the rise.

(Pictures on usage)

• Trends.Google.com

• Competitors' Sites

• Look at articles and content with the most:

• Views

• Comments

• Social shares

• Niche Forums

This is about researching on forums in your niche and finding out what are the most popular topics within your niche. Question and answer sites are a good start, but generally, you want to target forums where your potential clients are using.

Our Content Marketing Companies can easily explain to create content based on these topics and share them on forums, make them as valuable and informational as possible so it can benefit readers the most.

CHAPTER SEVEN

BUILDING AN EMAIL LIST

HOW TO BUILD AN EMAIL LIST FOR MARKETING?

Research shows that over 65% of marketing experts throughout the world ranked email as a best online marketing technique. When you build an email list you have a database of interested customers and prospects with whom you can directly communicate with about your products, services, and offers. Here are the 5 steps for building an email list for marketing.

1. Create something your target market needs

What information does your target market need? What problems are they trying to solve or what will make their life easier or more enjoyable? When you have decided on the best answer, put the details into something that you can give away to your audience for free. This could be a report, an eBook or a video series.

2. Set up a squeeze page

To build an email list for marketing you need to have a webpage that can capture email addresses. This is called a squeeze page. This is the page that will offer your prospects your free information in exchange for their email address. It will contain a box where people can enter and submit their email address to get access to your freebie. The squeeze page should have a nice graphic presentation. It needs to clearly describe the benefits of your freebie and how it can help your audience.

3. Set up email marketing software

It will become impossible for you to try and manually email your freebie to everyone who asks for it. Therefore you need to set up email marketing software to do this for you. This software is usually called an auto-responder. As well as collecting, managing, and segmenting your email database, it will enable you to automatically deliver a sequence of messages to your audience, develop newsletters and track your email marketing performance.

4. Drive traffic to your squeeze page

Your next step is to drive traffic to your squeeze page to get people to enter their email address onto squeeze page. There are two ways to do this. You can use paid traffic methods (e.g., pay per click marketing, solo ads, banner advertising, and social media advertising) or you can use free traffic methods (e.g., social media posts, blogging, video marketing, and search engine optimization). The option is to use a combination of both paid and free traffic.

5. Continue to provide value

As you build an email list for marketing you can't just continually send sales messages. You have to provide value to your subscribers. Ensure that there's a good balance between the times you email to push products and services and the times you're just sharing good information.

Reasons why you should start building an email list

Building an email list is essentially about creating a database of subscribers or followers. These people are potential consumers or customers. They have been qualified and would want to hear from you. They may not necessarily be endorsers or fans of everything you sell or offer but they are subscribers. They would receive your regular newsletters and follow everything that your brand does or intends to do. This following is not dissimilar to social media followers but the added advantage is the comprehensive informational exchanges you can have. Email is more detailed than social media posts and it is also more private. Both attributes make email marketing effectively and an email list more quintessential than you think.

1. An email list gives you a ready and waiting audience. You don't need to go out looking for a database or wait for the impending traffic. All your other marketing strategies will remain at play. The distinct advantage is that you can send out notifications or email updates and get the leads to respond. The ready audience will give a fillip to your traffic. They would share the email and also spread the word verbally. You would have direct responses in some cases that you can follow up on. Many people on your email list will take to social media to further spread the word which will assist your existing social media campaigns.

2. An email list is a dedicated base of potential customers. Social media following is a voluntary subscription which can waver at any given point in time. You can combine the two to have a more formidable social media presence and to expand your email list. Your social media followers who don't find a place on your email list will exponentially expand your database or your massive email database will help your social media following and hence enhance your influence.

CHAPTER EIGHT

DIFFERENT AFFILIATE MARKETING STRATEGIES

STEP-BY-STEP GUIDE OF AFFILIATE MARKETING STRATEGY

Making money from affiliate marketing is an art. Only writing a great product review or promoting a great product will not work to make any sales from your affiliate links. But you have to do many other things to make money from your affiliate links. Most of the Blog and website owners think that writing a great product review will work. But this is not enough. You need a perfect Affiliate Marketing strategy and must work on it to generate sales from your links.

HERE IS AN AFFILIATE MARKETING STRATEGY MODEL.

1. Take time (10-20 hours or even more) to choose a product to promote and write down a great, unique, and informative product review. This is very important.

2. Become an Affiliate of ClickBank, Amazon, or Commission Junction and generate an affiliate link for your product and put it on your review page and publish it on your website or a blog. Now, suppose if you are not the owner of any website or a blog then it's also perfectly alright. You can post your review on Squidoo, HubPages, Wetpaint, and other sites of that nature. Remember, all we need to do is publish your web page containing your affiliate link anywhere on the web and divert the web traffic towards it.

3. Link building. This is very important. Your Affiliate link is live now. The only thing you have to do is drive web traffic towards it (the more the better). For this, you have to create and publish the content on other popular websites on the Internet and then put a link of your affiliate page.

Examples are Squidoo, HubPages, WetPaint, YouTube, Xomba, eHow, WikiHow, Triond, Associated Content, Knol... etc... Post content having your affiliate link page link on each of the above websites.

4. Social Media. Try Facebook, Orkut, Twitter, Digg, Delicious, StumbleUpon & Reditt to divert more web traffic towards your affiliate links.

5. Now sit back and wait for the web traffic to accelerate. This will probably take 1 week to 15 days to drive web traffic towards your affiliate page. Once the web traffic comes toward your page, you will definitely make money. This is the Model of Affiliate Marketing strategy. Nobody will teach you this.

CHAPTER NINE

AFFILIATE MARKETING SECRETS

SECRETS OF SUCCESSFUL & PROFITABLE AFFILIATE MARKETING

In fact, after reading this chapter, you will understand that there is no secret at all. But everything about affiliate marketing revolves around the one basic principle and that is:

"To make money from affiliate marketing, you have to drive more web traffic towards your affiliate links."

The more web traffic you divert towards your affiliate links, the more sales it will generate and the more money you will make. It is this simple. And I believe you should not spend money on those products which claim that they are offering you some kind of secret.

Once you generate an affiliate link on your website or a blog, all you have to do is divert more and more web traffic towards those affiliate links by Twitter, Facebook, Digg, Delicious, StumbleUpon, Reddit, Articles Directories, SEO and many other things.

The more web traffic that you divert towards your affiliate links, the more sales it will generate. There is nothing secret about it. Even a School going Kid can do this to make 6 figures income every year by following this basic principle.

What is important is the proper mindset. You have to understand the principle and develop a mind frame and stick to it and prevent this mind frame by eroding from your emotions. That's it. This is all you have to do to make money from affiliate marketing.

You don't have to be a popular product review writer for this. Nor do you need to be the owner of an Authority Blog or a Website. Of course, if you are an owner of a successful blog or a website, it will be easy for you to make money from affiliate marketing because you can leverage your existing reader/customer base.

Thus, these are the secrets of successful affiliate marketing.

Now, take action and start making money.

Affiliate marketing eBooks

Should I Buy Affiliate Marketing eBooks?

You are here on this page probably because you have searched in Google for "Affiliate Marketing eBooks". I am sure that you have already gone through several websites and reviewed lots of books on affiliate marketing. But after watching literally hundreds of dollars of prices of those eBooks, you probably landed on this page.

Let me tell you that all of those eBooks are revolving around one basic core principle. This principle of making money from affiliate marketing will never even change in the near future. And that principle is:

"The key to successful affiliate marketing is WEB TRAFFIC. The more web traffic you divert towards your affiliate links from all around the web, naturally more sales it will generate and the more money you will make." Everything about affiliate marketing ultimately revolves around this simple but very basic principle. You will find literally millions of eBooks on this topic. All of those eBooks are written around this basic principle. So if you understand this basic principle, there is no need to buy any eBooks.

I have given you the principle of profitable affiliate links right? So now, you have to use your mind and figure out "How to divert more web traffic towards your affiliate links?" Let's discuss the example provided below:

Suppose I want to make money from affiliate marketing so what will I do? Well, first of all, I go to ClickBank.com and chose a product to sell. Well, I advise you to start from digital downloadable products first, this is because they are easy to deliver and the commission per sale is very high (20-75%) in these products.

OK so now I have chosen the product. So the next step is to create an affiliate link. So what will I do? Well, I will write a keyword rich product review having an affiliate link and post it on my blog or a website. Or any other social network that we have discussed earlier.

After that process, the affiliate link is on the web. It's life now. So your 50% of the job is complete. The rest of the 50% is to divert the web traffic towards your blog/social network/website page on which you have put the affiliate link. You can do this in several ways.

One is link building. There are 2 advantages of link building. One is that they will divert more traffic towards your web page as well as it will increase the search engine rankings of your web page so drive organic (Search engine) traffic.

For this, you have to write down and post content on various 5, 6, & 7-page rank articles directories such as:

EzineArticles

Squidoo

HubPages

WetPaint

YouTube

Xomba

Triond

Knol

eHow

You post articles on the above web directories. This is because Google simply loves and trusts these websites. So if each of these websites direct towards your web page having affiliate links, it will shoot up the page rank and thus more web traffic. Now, the second way to drive more traffic towards your websites is social networking and the third way is social media. Here are the examples:

Facebook

Orkut

MySpace

Digg

Delicious

Stumbleupon

Reddit

In short, you have to use your mind to find out more and more possible ways to divert the web traffic towards your affiliate links. Once you do all of this hard work. Just sit back and enjoy the steady passive income coming into your bank accounts.

FACEBOOK AFFILIATE MARKETING

HOW TO MAKE PASSIVE INCOME FROM FACEBOOK AFFILIATE MARKETING?

Affiliate marketing means selling other people's products from your web properties (Blogs & Websites) and getting a commission for each sale you make. You may ask: "How can I make money from Facebook Affiliate Marketing?" Well, As far as I know, there is not any direct method of doing affiliate marketing on Facebook. But let's go to the basics and find out how we use Facebook to do affiliate marketing?

What is the basic principle behind successful affiliate marketing?

Well, the basic principle of profitable affiliate marketing is - "The more web traffic you divert towards your Affiliate Links (Web pages having your affiliate links), the more sales your affiliate links will generate." This is the basic principle of affiliate marketing and every theory and techniques of profitable affiliate marketing revolve around this simple basic principle. Now, here we want to make money from Facebook Affiliate Marketing. So obviously, we need to find out the ways to divert traffic from Facebook to our affiliate links. Is this possible? Well, Yes. There are several ways by which you can divert the web traffic on Facebook to your affiliate links. Say, for Example, Fan pages, Comments, News Feeds, Facebook applications, Direct Advertising on Facebook... etc...

By these methods, you can easily divert web traffic from Facebook to your own web property having affiliate links. The more web traffic that you divert to your affiliate links, the more sales it will generate and thus the more money you will make.

However, there is only one problem with Social Networking sites traffic and that is the traffic of social networking sites is not a buyer's traffic. They are there on the Social Network for being Social. So making money from Social Network traffic is really a difficult task.

27

1. Own your own online affiliate marketing business

To own their own affiliate marketing business is the dream of many people, from all walks of life, both young and old. People, who dream about owning their own business, often dream that seductive, wonderful and tantalizing dream, the dream of being their own boss: the dream of becoming financially independent is so very real to them. The luxurious dream of not having to live from paycheck to paycheck, any longer.

The, almost real, dream of not having to get up each morning, at some unearthly hour: for five or six days every week. Unfortunately, in reality, it will always remain a dream unless people take action.

Many people just dream about not having to go to work and face their boss, whom they just plain don't like: and, their normal routine. Their routine is usually that same old familiar, soul-destroying, spirit-crushing, routine; which, depending on where in the world you live in, is at its worst during the winter months. It's the dreaded routine of having to get up in the morning, while it's still dark: then, when you get home at night again, finding it's still dark again. That's the routine that steadily wears you down; and, slowly but surely, kills people over the years.

Unfortunately for lots of people, who don't have any other options, this is the reality of their everyday working life, and it always will be unless they take action, and change that routine. That spirit draining, life sucking, mind-numbing, everyday routine that destroys their happiness; and, sometimes, their very soul. Their routine of waking up, getting out of bed and taking a shower, of eating a hurried breakfast, gulping down a quick cup of coffee; then dashing out, maybe, in the rain or snow, to the dreaded daily commute, or maybe an hour or more in heavy traffic.

Ask yourself if your own routine of arriving at your 'j.o.b'; and, for the next eight hours, being at the beck and call of your boss, is really what you want to settle for? This, for five or six days, each and every week; and for, maybe, the next forty or fifty years: for the rest of your life, until you die? I ask this because there is a much more attractive and much, much, more lucrative alternative: but, unless you do something about it, and take action, nothing will change!

Given the above harsh truths, it's no wonder that so many peoples' minds yearn for the freedom that owning their own online business can give them. Well, guess what, for those people who don't have a 'slave mentality'; for those who dream of living life on their own terms, and not having to answer to their boss, you can do just that. Because, with the advent of the new online digital economy, freedom is yours for the taking. Freedom now awaits people just like you.

For those who are possessed of an entrepreneurial spirit, and are willing to invest in themselves, and learn, there are now online business opportunities, such as buying and selling: or affiliate marketing, which allows people who fit the above description, to work from the comfort of their own homes.

Affiliate marketing can enable you to travel; and, to be able to work from your own kitchen table, or anywhere else in the world. You can even work from the beach if you wish.

Yes, there are some people who will hesitate, and start thinking about the responsibilities of owning their own business. About how they would be able to manage to do all of the different jobs that owning their own business will bring with it? I know that scares the living daylights out of a lot of timid people! There

28

are some people who lack the courage, and tend to shy away from, even the very thought of, owning their own businesses: mostly because of all the different skills that are needed!

Those fears are ungrounded, kick them out, they should not be allowed to stop you owning your own business. The chief culprit responsible for those fears is the past mind conditioning that all of us have experienced, for most of our past lives. To give you an example of this, let's say that, if I asked you this question, 'Can you could finish this well known old saying?', "If you want something doing right, 'di dah de dah di dah'." I'll bet that you would very likely be able to give me the correct answer; because, as most of us know, we've been taught that the final words of this sentence are "do it yourself". This saying was credited to one Charles-Guillaume Etienne, who was a 19th Century French writer. Since then, it's been passed on, over and over again; ad nauseum, by well-meaning parents, coaches, gurus and anyone else in the world who teaches self-reliance.

For over two hundred years it has been gobbled up, without a second thought, and passed on by their disciples: also by their children, their followers, and their minions. We've all been mind-conditioned into accepting as being the truth, the old saying that, "If you want something doing right you must do it yourself."

At best, this is suspect advice because, when you think about that saying, it's probably one of the worst pieces of advice to ever have become a universal cliche. Not least because, unless you're an absolutely superb expert at that particular, "something", that you need doing, how can you be sure that you are going to have the necessary skills that will enable you to "do it right" when you try to do it yourself?

Most human beings are highly proficient at only a handful of skills. So, for 99.999% of those "something's", that you want doing right, isn't it better to find someone else to do it for you?

Someone who really is highly qualified, and very talented, at whatever it is that you want doing: and, definitely, not to keep on slaving away, trying to doing it yourself.

In the new global digital economy, there are people who earn their full-time living working online; people whom you can hire to do anything you need doing. For example, let's say that you need someone to write great copy for you; or, to design and build you a highly converting website and make sure that your site is optimized, so it will rank highly on the search engine results.

There are many hundreds of other 'something's' that you might need doing; but, on the plus side, there are literally thousands of highly qualified experts online who are competing for our business, and who will do those 'something's' for us: starting from as little as $5.00. So, when 'hired help' is available very cheaply, it's not very smart to try and do these things yourself.

You should stick to doing the things that you really are good at. There are some really great online, work from home businesses; which, if you are willing to work at, will enable you to make you a very good income and will give you the freedom to live life on your own terms. A life that can bring you very rich financial rewards, and will enable you to have the time to travel the world and meet new people. People who are of the same, entrepreneurial, go-ahead, mindset as you are. You don't have to do everything yourself, in fact, it's not very smart to even try.

One of the misconceptions that people have about owning their own business is that you need to have a huge amount of start-up capital in order to do it: well, a misconception is exactly what that is, a wrong idea, a misunderstanding. Because you definitely do NOT need a huge pile of cash to get started on the pathway to owning your own business, your freedom giving, liberating and very profitable, own business: in fact, you can get started for less than $50. Nor, do you have to try doing everything yourself; there are very successful people who are willing to mentor you, to train you and, virtually, 'hold your hand, along the road to financial freedom.

It will pay handsome dividends for you to think about all the "something's" that you may be currently struggling to do by yourself, which you should really be delegating to someone else. Just imagine, if you owned your own online business today, ask yourself, would you follow that dodgy piece of 19th-century advice, "If you want something done right, do it yourself?" Take a look at the list below.

• Creating products to sell

• Sourcing products to sell

• Generating traffic

• Converting traffic

• Phone sales

• Customer service

• Website design

• Business accounting

• Tax returns

• Staff payroll

WOW! I don't know about you, but I get the mental picture of somebody in a circus, rushing to and fro, desperately trying to keep those plates spinning around, on the tops of bamboo canes? How many people would even have the necessary skills, or the time, to efficiently handle all of the ten tasks above: very few I would imagine.

However, you can have someone do all of those things for you; and, that's what you should look for when you think about owning your online business. That, and for the smallest possible start-up cash outlay and the ability to automate your own business, in order to free up your time, so that you can enjoy the money you're making. That's what you should be looking for when you begin to think about owning your own online business. You should only try to learn from people who are more successful than you are; and, then you really can actually start living your dream.

You're at a fork in the road now; and, if you take the wrong path, on the left, and do nothing; then, tomorrow, you'll be stuck in just the same place where you're now at. You'll be living life by someone else's rules, and making money for someone else, with no hope of ever enjoying financial freedom. Here's the honest truth; you can resent the wealthy or you can join them, but only if you take the right path. If you have the courage, you can take that path on the right. Here it is, below: The path to change... To a better life... A life full of Big Paydays... and a life with no "money worries."

CHAPTER TEN

MISTAKES TO AVOID

We all make mistakes. It's part of the process of learning. But some mistakes are greater than others. Take affiliate marketing as an example. It's considered to be the easiest and quickest way to make money online. Yet for some people, it just doesn't work. The concept is pretty straightforward. As an affiliate marketer, you earn commissions by promoting other people's products or services on the internet. You find a product you like, promote it to a target audience, and earn a piece of the profit for each sale that you make.

So where do people go wrong? Here are 5 common affiliate marketing mistakes to avoid.

1. Don't expect instant success. Affiliate marketing online can generate revenue fairly quickly. Having said that, a life-changing income won't happen overnight. It takes time to build an audience and a customer base. If you accept that making money with affiliate marketing is a legitimate business model you'll realize that you have to put appropriate business strategies in place to succeed and these take time to implement.

2. Don't target a large generic audience. You'll have more success if you target a smaller niche market rather than a massive market. For example, 'weight loss' is a massive market. But 'weight loss for women over 40' is much more niche and targeted. The most successful affiliates directly target a specific niche market in which a product or service that is designed for people in that market.

3. Don't give up too quickly. Affiliate marketing is a competitive business. And many people give up right when they are on the brink of developing success. You can make a profit from affiliate marketing but you need to take a long-term view and commit to a least 1 or 2 years to build up your business.

4. Don't promote anything and everything. Restrict yourself to a handful of high-value products that have good reviews by customers. Don't just promote all and every affiliate program that pays out high commissions. Promoting anything and everything, with a new offer going out to your email list or website visitors every day, is a quick way to get dismissed by your audience.

5. Don't be like every other affiliate. Don't forget that there are many other affiliates promoting the same products and services you are. To encourage people to buy from you, rather than another affiliate, create a bonus, such as an eBook, report or video that someone would be happy to pay for. By doing this you add value to the purchase, something that the majority of other affiliate marketers never do.

CONCLUSION

Affiliate marketing is a terrific way to start making money from the internet. You don't need to develop your own products or services, keep any stock, deal with payment systems or organize deliveries. You promote products on behalf of another business and when you make a sale, you get paid a commission.

The problem is that a lot of people already know this. That means there's a lot of affiliates out there who are most likely seeking to sell the same products as you.

To succeed

1. Choose your niche carefully. It's important that you put some thought and homework into your niche before you start trying to sell affiliate products. To start with, do you have a real interest in your chosen niche or industry? If you're trying to sell something that holds very little interest for you, you're in a negative position before you even get started and it's unlikely that you'll keep with it for very long.

On the other hand, it's also important to test that your chosen niche is profitable. Are people buying the type of product that you want to promote? Before you start to promote products and services as an affiliate, check out its conversion rates. This means how many potential consumers actually turn into buyers.

2. Use reputable affiliate programs. As an affiliate marketer, you're promoting another the products or services of another business. But, with regards to your prospective customers, they will think that they are buying from you. Therefore, make sure that you're associating yourself with reputable affiliate companies that have integrity stand behind their products and support their affiliates.

3. Use the right kind of affiliate links. Your objective is to get someone to click through on your affiliate link. This is the unique URL link that an affiliate program will use to keep track of your sales. There are all kinds of links you can use to get someone to visit a product's sales page. These include embedded text, banners, search boxes and other less common methods.

If you want to actually sell products or find clients, you need to research all the choices and make the right decision for what you're trying to do.

4. Have your own website and email list. You can start marketing affiliate without having your own website. You basically send prospects directly to a product owner's sales page. Having said that, if that prospect doesn't buy anything, you've lost them forever. On the other hand, if your prospects are associated to your website and have signed up with your email list, if they don't buy a specific offer today, you can tempt them with something else in the future.

Creating your own affiliate marketing website isn't as difficult as you might think, and there are several easy to use website platforms that can get you online quickly and efficiently. Companies are happy to pay commissions to people just like you, in return for selling their products and services. You have the potential to make a great income when you choose the right niche, stay committed, and understand your audience.

HOW TO IDENTIFY THE NEEDS OF YOUR POTENTIAL CUSTOMERS

When developing your new online business, you need to be able to identify your potential customers. The steps that you can follow are to develop a profile of your potential customers. This profile should include ethnicity, age range, income level, occupation, religion, and gender. More specific considerations would include their level of education, internet surfing habits, special interests, buying habits, and needs.

Once you have developed a profile of your potential customers, you need to know what their actual needs and wants are related to the product or service that you will sell. Can you show to yourself that the product or service that you are offering will solve a problem, meet a need, save time or money? In addition, can you show that your product or service will help them achieve a goal or offer a source of further education?

As you begin to develop your website, use the information that you have gathered from your customer profile. You will create a more successful website if you understand your target audience. You can use a combination of videos, graphics, text, and audios to specifically engage your target audience. The better that you understand your target audience, the more successful you will be. Knowing your target audience will also aid you in better usage of your marketing money. Your funds will be best spent if you promote your business to reach that segment of people that your business is targeting.

Another idea is to develop a list of all of the reasons why a person in your targeted audience will want your product or service. You will understand your targeted audience even better if you compile a list of all the reasons why someone should not want your product or service. Then using this list of negative reasons, develop a sales method or solution that will counteract each of these objections. Using these solutions, convert them to a method that you can use online.

Other solutions to understanding your targeted audience can be in the form of questionnaires to your customers or performing marketing research. Keep foremost in your mind, that when designing your website, it should be tailored to attract your targeted audience.

GOOD LUCK!

PART 2:

START YOUR

OWN BUSINESS

Learn How Successful Entrepreneurs Can Turn Any Idea into a Profit

By K. Connors

TABLE OF CONTENT

INTRODUCTION

Whether you're struggling to find employment or simply wanting to be your own boss, looking to start your own business is exactly the right thing to do for many people. However, I'm not here to sugar coat it for you. On the road to success lies many shattered dreams and tattered ambition. This information will help you give yourself the best chance of success. Ahead of anything else is making that first move. Though starting your own business is never an easy challenge, it is important to be aware that the perfect moment is never likely to come. There is no time like the present. Possessing the focus and the ability to shrug off lingering worries and press ahead is often the key to success.

Having a particular market to explore, perhaps a niche area not presently filled will help. If so, the earlier you start the better things will most likely be. Being aware of the local climate is essential since even seemingly inaccessible industries will present excellent opportunities. Of course, coming up with a unique idea or breaking into a new market can be incredibly difficult - and is where many new businesses fail.

Sometimes though, as the old adage goes, you fail to see the wood for the trees, so considering things that may be staring you right in the face is important. Look at whether there are any professional services that local businesses are not being provided with. If provided for, are the current services really up to the task? Perhaps start your own business on that basis.

If in employment already, consider if there are any suppliers that management is consistently complaining about. Ask yourself if you could do better. Many individuals attain personal success by first identifying a problem, and then working to solve it.

With a plan in place, knowing whether you already possess the necessary skills, or have yet to attain them, is important. You most likely already have one of the most important skills - the drive to start your own business. If you do not have the actual skills to deliver the product, then working out a way to attain them is the next step.

Consider whether there is a franchisor offering a franchise opportunity in the business sector you are interested in.

Respected franchises are clearly doing something right, have excellent training in place, business knowledge, and a proven model to give you the great start that can feel impossible with brand new enterprises. Most importantly though, a good franchisor provides expertise and essential support. In essence, it is your own business with the support of a successful chain. From helping to locate a viable area in which to start a business, to assisting with the logistics of setting up the premises, there is much to be gained from being part of a franchise.

Every business needs funding, and getting this in place is often the toughest challenge. Not securing the financing can end many of the best-planned ambitions, though lenders are eager to invest in strong opportunities. Again, franchisees with a proven business model can help secure funding far easier than start-ups, making it an increasingly viable option if you want to start your own business.

REASONS TO START YOUR OWN BUSINESS

People all over the world are searching for new ways to make money. However, they are somewhat confused on the direction they should take. In addition, some people are confused as to why people are going the "entrepreneurial" route instead of the educational route. In my opinion, I believe that someone should exercise all opportunities to make money. Whether it is going to school or starting your own business, I believe that this world is too insecure to have only one source of income.

Below are reasons why some people are looking into starting their own businesses.

1. Make your own hours

2. You get to call the shots

3. You can create your work environment

4. You can pursue your own passion

5. You get to create your own ideas from scratch

Although people are looking into starting their own business, home businesses are on the rise because of the convenience to the owner. Not to mention some of the tax benefits as well.. People love the ability to discipline themselves and work in their pajamas. In the real world, most employees are at the mercy of the companies who employ them. If your child is sick, in most cases, you must still go to work. In the workforce, you are only allowed a certain amount of days you are able to call off.

Here Are Some More Reasons

6. You are able to meet new people

7. You get to build your own team

8. You get to help people

9. You are able to invest in yourself

10. Earning potential is much higher

11. You become financially independent

12. You get tax benefits

13. You get to connect with your customers

14. You get to avoid boring tasks

15. You get to discover new fields

16. You get to become a mentor and inspire others

Is it possible for you to earn a living through owning your own business? 6 out of 10 businesses fail within the first year due to lack of education. Luckily for you, there are successful companies that offer free advice on the proper steps to take to create a lucrative business.

Although there are many resources available on the internet, the most important thing for you to note is, you must take the time to figure out what industry you would like to be involved in and what are your strengths as a person. If you are able to figure out who you are as a person, you will be able to find the perfect niche to be involved in.

CHAPTER ONE

JUST DO IT

For those who dream of having your own business, you're not alone. It's estimated that about 600,000 new businesses are started every year. In the event you're one of the many thousands of individuals trying to determine how to start your own business, this is a great place to begin. Starting your own business offers many benefits - more freedom, the potential to earn more, significant tax advantages, the opportunity to arrange your work life in a manner that works best for you, the possibility of building a beneficial asset you'll be able to sell or give away to your children. The list goes on and on.

Of course, there are challenges and risks, as well. But with some good planning and just a little education, you'll be able to reduce these dramatically. In truth, there has never been a greater time in history to start your own business. The Internet and everything it offers - just about limitless access to information, the power to simply and quickly talk with others, prompt access to specialists in every field, the chance to leverage your effort and time - make exploring how to start your own business easier and more efficient than ever.

Many people make the mistake of leaping into some sort of business without closely considering what they're doing and how to best do it. That's where sites like this can help. There are so many different types of companies out there right now - on-line businesses like Web marketing, on-line retailing, etc.; networking, advertising, franchises, etc. Making an attempt to resolve what to pursue might be overwhelming, especially because so many companies are hyped up with advertising and promotions.

The best advice is to do your homework, read books and others like it. Examine various kinds of businesses. Read opinions from those who are already doing it. Find packages that offer step-by-step instruction or training. Take some time to do it right, and you will be a lot happier and successful in the long run.

There are plenty of resources on-line - useful websites, informative articles, tons of ideas and advice.

All right there at your disposal, whenever you want them. Home businesses have been becoming more and more important throughout years. If the events of the past few years have taught us nothing else, they have proven that there isn't as much job security out there anymore as we would hope. The only security, the only guaranteed future, is the one you create for yourself.

Don't let another year pass with anything to show but an unfulfilled dream. Get started learning how to start your own business at this time! There is no cause to delay. There is an abundance of information accessible all over the place; anyone can do it!

Bear in mind, there's no time like the present! And no better future than the one you create for yourself. Start educating yourself on how to start your own business today! Just do it.

THE FIRST STEP IN STARTING YOUR OWN BUSINESS

The first step in starting your own business is to perform a thorough research on the kind of business to set up. It is through research that you will be able to identify the business opportunities you can engage in. After you have found out the various areas you can engage in you will be able to choose the area that suits you best. The main reason why many businesses fail shortly after commencing is because of a failure to perform a serious research on a business idea before implementing it.

By researching you are able to understand consumer needs, tastes and preferences. By doing so you will be able to provide what the consumers require. This would mean more sales resulting in high profits which are the objective of almost all businesses. The other reason why research is the first step in starting your own business is that through research, one is able to see both the pros and cons of entering certain niche markets.

The best location of your business is another important factor one will learn after conducting research. It is also very important for one to research before commencing a business in order to find the appropriate distribution channels. This is because you may have the right product and charge the right prices, but it may fail to reach the intended audience.

For your business to perform well it must be properly promoted. The correct advertising technique must be adopted in order to reach the targeted group. For all of the above to be achieved, the correct choice of promotion must be made. It is almost impossible to get the choice right without performing research, and that is why it is the first step in starting your own business. There are certain types of businesses that are very heavily taxed and charged by the government. In order to avoid such mistakes, the proper research must be conducted on various government policies and regulations before setting up the business.

Moreover, before beginning a business of your own, you must clearly understand all that it entails before you jump right in; the kind of licenses or permits you will need to obtain and the kind of products or services that are illegal and as such should be avoided. You will only learn this when you conduct your research. It is, therefore, necessary that you undertake this research as the first step in starting your own business.

CHAPTER TWO

DO I BUILD FROM SCRATCH OR BUY A FRANCHISE?

There are literally millions of people who attempt to start up some form of business each year around the globe. From those millions, hundreds of thousands succeed in starting it, and a far fewer number succeed in maintaining that business. For most, they are deterred and are ultimately unsuccessful. For others, their businesses do start up, but plummet within the first year. The lucky few who make it owe their success to an unlimited number of factors. For the potential business owners of the world, one way to improve your chances of success is to buy pre-owned. Instead of starting up your own business from scratch, buying an existing business or business idea can really help you be successful. There are many benefits in buying and taking over an existing business.

One of the largest deterrents of a new business is the idea of building it from scratch. You have to mold and perfect your business idea and formulate plans, work to gather a niche, attack the market, compete and stand out and ultimately cross your fingers and hope for the best; whereas, with a pre-existing business, most of that groundwork is already covered and perfected.

You can purchase a pre-existing business in a number of different ways. Maybe you have your eye on a restaurant or bar that is going out of business and you think you have the right recipe to get it back on its feet. Perhaps the owner of a business is retiring and wants to sell off his or her business. Or, you can purchase a franchise and take over the responsibility that way.

Regardless of how you acquire an existing business, the advantages are evident. For starters, the business is ready for immediate operations. Someone else has already gotten the business up and running. This also means that you should experience some quick cash flow, especially from existing inventory and/or clients. You can possibly generate income from the first day. Your customer base is also solidified. Instead of seeking out a new market, you can simply work to broaden your existing one. Since the business has a track record, the finances will be easier to maintain.

When it comes to competition, you can buy your way into a business that already has the market cornered. Some disadvantages exist, as well, so it's not all wine and roses here.

The cost of purchasing an existing business can sometimes be higher since you're paying for an operating business. The owner could have kept some serious problems hidden from you in order to sell off quickly. If you're a strong-willed person, you may meet some resistance from existing personnel within the business.

You could be dealing with obsolete goods. Apart from the higher costs, however, a bit of research into the business you wish to buy can reveal the rest of these flaws. With a little bit of work, you can correct any problems before you settle into your new business.

THINGS TO KNOW ABOUT FRANCHISING AND FRANCHISE OPPORTUNITIES

Franchising is proving to be the most resilient and effective way to undertake large-scale expansions. Many corporations, particularly those based in the U.S., have undertaken significant expansion and to some extent diversification through this route. The fact that both the franchiser and franchisee have a stake in the success of the store or the outlet coupled with the fact that the appointed franchisees are usually indigenous people with good understanding of local laws, it already has the interest of all parties involved; this coupled with the international and modern best practices of the franchise enables scope for considerable synergy.

Franchise cost: Franchise cost generally depends on the following factors,

1.　FRANCHISE FEE: It is necessary to understand all services that are included in this fee because some franchises include land survey, expertise and skill development cost, and their trademark and logo cost, whereas some charge the franchise fee as a cost for just using the trademark and logo.

2.　LEGAL FEES: Since the transactions are fairly large, you may have to consult your legal team to advise you about UFOC (Uniform Franchise Offering Circular). It is important to understand that since every franchise outlet is different and hence there may be a variation in costs.

3.　WORKING CAPITAL: As with any business it is important to keep your business well capitalized for day to day transactions.

4.　INITIAL SETUP COSTS INCLUDING INVENTORY AND SUPPLIES NEEDS TO BE CONSIDERED

Franchise Opportunities: As with any other business there are a lot of franchise opportunities depending on your budget. There are franchise opportunities which cater to a wide range of budget estimates and also cut across various sectors, so there needs to be a balance between what you like or desire and what you can afford.

WHY GO FOR FRANCHISING?

If you are tired of your corporate job, and if you no longer wish to operate under someone else, you can either run a start-up of your own, or you can purchase a franchise. If you decide to run your own startup, you have to consider the risks involved. Firstly, you will be starting from scratch. So, you will have to build your brand name from the bottom up. You have to build a customer base from scratch as well, as you will be a new business on the market. In addition, you will have to break even with the high costs involved in running a start up.

If the risks involved in a start up leave you disgruntled, you may consider buying a franchise instead. When you buy a franchise, you are actually buying the business model of an existing company to serve a specific locality. For instance, if you know of a successful fast food chain that is open to franchising, you can buy the franchise and sell their goods under their banner and retain the majority of the profits. You function exactly as the parent company functions.

The main advantage with franchising is that you do not have to shoulder as many risks. Usually, the parent company is a well-known company. So, the brand name is already established. The brand is likely to have a loyal customer base in the area you plan to serve as well. The market is already there, you only have to service it. Where there is an existing market for your services, there you will also find profit to be made.

Secondly, the training for the staff is provided by the franchise at a fixed cost, in addition to the initial price of the franchise. You do not have to conduct any training. All you have to do is focus on running the business successfully.

Even though you have bought the business model of a company, you are not completely answerable for your work. As long as you maintain the brand image of the company, you are only answerable to yourself with regards to your hard work and discipline.

If you are interested in franchising, there are many businesses for sale that you can look into. Franchise opportunities are increasing as more and more companies and individuals are realizing the profitability of the venture in the long run.

ADVANTAGES OF BUYING A FRANCHISE BUSINESS

There are many advantages to buying a franchise business, especially a well-known one, rather than building a business from scratch. A disadvantage of owning a franchise is that you will not have the satisfaction of saying, "This business was my idea." However, the main reason for starting your own business is to make money and gain independence, and you are more likely to succeed with a franchise than with a business idea of your own.

One of the key advantages of buying a franchise is that you hit the ground running. There is no need, as with a new and unknown business, to invest heavily in building awareness of your products and services. Most franchises, even lesser-known ones, have achieved this already at a local if not the national level. Most people are already aware of what the business has to offer and provided it is a popular franchise, are "prepped" to feel positive about your business.

Another advantage of buying a franchised business is that you can do things the right way - the way that works - from day one. Typically, it takes several years for a new business to find its feet in terms of what works and what doesn't. Mistakes cost money. When you buy a franchise you also buy an entire system of practices, procedures, and policies that are a proven formula for success. In other words, you can start making money right away instead of losing it on the learning curve.

When you buy a franchise, owners and staff receive valuable training from the franchise which ensures your business meets customer expectations from the start. Again, this enables you to avoid a costly learning curve and immediately capitalize on the popularity of your franchise.

Another advantage to buying a franchise is that there is no need to spend a fortune on advertising and promotions. Firstly, your business is already well-known. Secondly, the franchise will supply all the necessary signage. Thirdly, franchisers often run major campaigns which individual outlets could never afford. All you need to do is spend what you need to spend to keep the customers coming and build on existing popularity.

A final advantage - and it is an important one - is that by buying a franchise you are buying an easy option for independence. Despite initial excitement and enthusiasm, the stresses and strains of starting a business from scratch, with little or no support, often prove too much for new business owners. Once again, the purpose of owning your own business is essential to gain ownership of your own life. As you can see, given the choice between your own idea for a business - risky and costly in more ways than one - there are clear advantages to buying a franchise business.

BENEFITS OF BEING PART OF FRANCHISING OVER STARTING FROM SCRATCH

Owning your own business is an attractive prospect for many people, but it does carry a great deal of risk with it. There are many advantages to working within a franchise rather than starting your own business.

Being part of a franchise gives a greater sense of security for the business owner, as you have the backing of a much larger parent company behind you. They can give you access to professional business advice, training, and resources not normally available for your traditional business owner.

PRIMARY BENEFITS

1. LEARN TO RUN THE BUSINESS EFFECTIVELY: Being part of a franchise team gives you access to mentoring and advice from those that know how to run a business effectively. You will be able to use a tried and trusted formula when running that franchise and have confidence that it is a winning model.

   Even if you lack experience in specific facets of a business, owning a franchise will allow you to plug these knowledge gaps and gain the required skills quickly.

2. LOW BUSINESS RISK: It is in the interest of the parent company for the individual franchise to succeed. For this reason, there is a dramatically lower risk involved than when starting a company from scratch. Franchise businesses have a 2-3 times greater chance of success than other small businesses starting up.

3. REDUCED RUNNING COSTS: As a member of a franchise group you can benefit from the bulk buying power of the parent company and save money on day-to-day running costs. If you are keen on starting up your own company, make sure you research the possibility of a franchise business first.

4. REPUTATION BUILDING: Trading under an already established name will take a lot of the work out of brand and reputation building, which can take a significant chunk of your marketing budget, especially initially.

5. A BUSINESS MODEL: While starting your own business means you will have to learn and form everything from scratch, franchising offers you a working business model for running a business. Franchising is a network of interdependent business relationships that allows a number of people to share a brand identification, a successful method of doing business, and a strong marketing and distribution system.

6. SAFETY IN PROVEN SYSTEMS: For the franchisee, franchising is about risk reduction and safety. You trade in the freedom associated with being an independent owner for an opportunity to become part of a group of people committed to building a brand and dominating markets using a common, tested operating system.

No more guesswork about the most effective way to build your business: The franchise provides a proven method (the operating system), a brand or trademark recognized by customers, and technical support so you won't have to reinvent the wheel to be successful.

On the other hand, you provide the capital to expand the brand faster than the franchise can by itself as well as the management talent to run the business and execute the operating system.

7. PREDICTABLE RESULTS: Being part of a franchise system should also provide group buying power to cut your operating expenses, faster growth due to tested marketing programs, predictable results based on your adherence to the operating system and less risk of your invested capital. The trade-offs for you are the fees you pay the franchise for the operating license and the restrictions imposed by the franchise on the method of operating the business.

THE BOTTOM LINE

The bottom line is whether you would like to run your business your own way or own a well-known branch while adhering to a working business model with rules set by someone else. Your answer to this question will tell you whether franchising is for you.

ADVANTAGES OF STARTING YOUR BUSINESS FROM SCRATCH

Starting a business of your own with an idea, and a bit of imagination allows you to be your own boss. Starting a business can be a difficult decision if you are not sure if you have what it really takes to be an entrepreneur. Don't worry; everyone starting out, in building any type of business has those same thoughts to some degree.

First, you should think about how you can start a business. You can start a business from scratch, and this means without buying any idea or model that is already established. This is one of the riskiest paths to self-employment, but one that many have done successfully in the past. It may also be the most satisfying and fulfilling should you succeed. Every day new restaurants, retail outlets, stores, service centers and the like are being established, fresh and new to the market. This is your clean slate, where you can start your own reputation; your own name in the industry, and you put forth your own thoughts and ideas into the business world.

The advantage to your own start-up business is you will learn from your mistakes, making changes along the way. If you were to hire the wrong type of employees, or if you have the wrong location, you can change these things. You make the decisions; no set patterns or ideas you must follow to get additional sales for your business.

Although, building a business is a challenge. There is much to learn and overcome. Nevertheless, it can be very rewarding both personally and financially. Knowing why you want to start a business in the first place can help you stay focused and keep you moving forward through adversity.

BY STARTING YOUR OWN BUSINESS, YOU:

1. ACQUIRE NEW SKILLS: Starting a business from scratch offers you the opportunity for constant and never-ending improvement. It allows you to enhance and acquire new skills like marketing, management, productivity, communication, delegation, research, product development, technical skills, and a variety of others. Although this can be overwhelming at times, the effect is that you are better prepared for uncertainty and change because you have worked to broaden your skill sets and knowledge. As a result, you have more options at your disposal. This is particularly important in a dynamic and uncertain world.

2. SHARPEN YOUR CREATIVITY: To start a business from scratch, you must use the power of your mind to create. Whether you create an actual product, marketing materials, training for your team, come up with new strategies, try new techniques, and so on, a business will force you to sharpen your creativity and become more innovative. It is just a natural process of engaging in a productive endeavor. The more you apply your mind to a creative project, the more you will build your creative thinking muscles.

3. BUILD YOUR OWN ASSETS: Starting a business from scratch gives you the unique ability to create assets that you own. Whether it is a product, a service, intellectual property, or a brand, your business is an asset that has value and can potentially generate income for years to come. You can, in turn, reinvest the income you generate into enhancing your skill sets, growing your business, or purchasing other income producing assets. There is something very powerful about creating and owning your own assets. Starting your own business gives you the means to do that.

4. IDENTIFY AND SOLVE PROBLEMS: The purpose of a business is to solve problems and satisfy the needs, wants, and desires of others. Starting your own business forces you to become more observant and identify the problems that people face on a daily basis. As a business owner, you now have an incentive to solve problems and meet people's needs.

The more you practice identifying problems and coming up with solutions, the better you become at this process. As a result, the better you become at serving others through your business.

5. OFFER YOUR OWN PRODUCTS AND SERVICES THAT SERVE THE COMMUNITY: Through your business, you have the privilege of making a positive impact in the lives of others. By providing value through your products and/or services, you have the potential to help solve people's problems and meet their needs. A lot of satisfaction can be derived from knowing that you are making a positive contribution to the lives others by serving them through your products and services. This is yet another appealing reason to start your own business from scratch.

Now that you have become aware of more reasons to start a business from scratch, the next step becomes how to get started. Of course, there are many ways to go about doing this. One of the easiest and fastest ways to get started is to use a simple marketing system that has already been created. The advantage of using such a system is that you don't have to invest the time or the money to create another one. You can simply focus on learning marketing skills and generating an income right away while you develop more advanced skills and clarify exactly what you want to focus on in the meantime.

You can then take the income that you generate and reinvest it into your business education and the tools you need to grow your business even further.

Whether you choose to franchise a business or start from scratch, that doesn't mean you always have to stick with that one business model forever. The way we become financially independent is to have multiple streams of income. Many franchise owners dabble in multiple business ideas once their franchised business is on auto pilot. Many "start from scratch" business owners learn the do's and don'ts of owning a business the hard way through mistakes, thus making a franchise opportunity a walk in the park for them.

CHAPTER THREE

STARTING YOUR OWN BUSINESS: DO IT RIGHT

WHAT ARE YOU GOOD AT? WHAT DO YOU LIKE?

It is perhaps the true "American Dream" to leave your job working for someone else and start your own business? The idea is that not only do you have more control over your time commitment, pay, and the types of customers you deal with - but it also enables people to engage in an activity they actually have a passion for. However, just having that passion is not enough to make a venture successful. It takes thorough planning and a major time investment.

1. CHOOSE SOMETHING THAT YOU HAVE A PASSION FOR: This venture is still a job, and you will be less likely to put forth the requisite effort and care if you are not emotionally attached to the business.

2. DO YOUR RESEARCH INTO THE MARKET YOU ARE LOOKING TO GET INTO: Unless you have a new invention or can revolutionize a current process, you need to find a niche market in which you can differentiate yourself from every other similar business.

3. ALWAYS CONSULT A LEGAL PROFESSIONAL: Preferably one that specializes in business start-ups or an accounting professional. They will be the best source of guidance when it comes to selecting a business structure and naming issues, as well as state and local licensing issues.

4. STICK TO WHAT YOU KNOW BEST AND DO NOT TRY TO DO EVERYTHING YOURSELF: If you are not good at handling finances, then hire an accountant or bookkeeper. If you are not graphically inclined, then hire a design firm to create your logo and marketing tools. It is always cheaper to spend the money and have it done right from the beginning than it is to fix a problem over and over again.

5. DO NOT RUSH. Take your time and make sure that everything is to your specification. You need to be 100% ready for business from the day the doors first open.

6. NETWORK. Tell everyone you know about your business. Word of mouth is the cheapest and most effective form of marketing. Also, solicit their opinions on everything from the name of the business, to the logo design, to the promotions you will be having. Having outsiders who are less biased critique your business leads to more honest reviews and will most likely reflect the public's opinion as well.

7. Make sure to budget enough money for advertising & marketing, as well as overhead, legal & accounting, insurance, etc.

8. Have patience. Success is not an overnight occurrence and generally will take much time, work, and effort.

9. Talk to people who are successful in the industry you are looking to enter (although try to choose people who you will not be in direct competition with). Try to pick their brains as much as you can without being intrusive. Many successful people are more than happy to share their stories and how the got to where they are.

10. Join professional associations suh as the local Chamber of Commerce and networking groups. Form strategic alliances with others who offer similar yet distinctive products or services to gain mutual benefit.

11. Don't be afraid to take calculated risks; just don't be reckless. There's no reward without risk, but don't take that risk without weighing the pros and cons first.

Above all else, surround yourself with positive people who will support you and your ideas.

This list is by no means complete, and in my estimation can never be considered complete. There are too many things that need consideration, and everything varies by experience level and industry. However, this is a good starting point.

WHAT ARE YOU GOOD AT? WHAT DO YOU LIKE?

Step 1: MAKE UP YOUR MIND:

It all starts here. Decide that you're ready: Say "I'm ready to run my own business." Find a spot in your house or rent/lease a location. Pick a day on your calendar.

Step 2: PICK AN AREA

Maybe right this minute you have no idea what to do. That's fine. Keep looking; just don't take a decade doing it. The best place to start is, of course, your hobby. Turn your hobby of scrapbooking, soap making, or model trains into a profit. You're not the only one with this interest. In this day and age, you can find a niche market in almost anything. Use your hobby as a business idea.

Step 3: MAKE IT LEGAL

Now, this is the part that often deters many aspiring entrepreneurs; don't let it! Your government wants you to run your own business and have set up tremendous incentives for you. The Small Business Association (SBA) provides a "Starting Your Business" section of their website that can give everything you need to know about the legal aspects of starting a business.

One last food for thought: Experts believe that the next wave of millionaires is likely to be dominated by small-business entrepreneurs; you can be one of them.

FINDING THE PERFECT IDEA

The answer to this question is that the perfect idea probably doesn't exist. Your aim should be to choose an idea that is practical and workable, given your skills and experience, and your long-term goals. It should also be an idea that fires your enthusiasm and something that you can really believe in! Charles J. Duell, the Commissioner of the US patent office in 1899 once said "Everything that can be invented has already been invented". Boy, was he wrong.. The same thing has probably been said today once or twice, and it would still be just as wrong.

Some new business owners find it hard to settle on a single business idea because they are worried about missing out on new opportunities or narrowing their options too early on. But remember, even when you have started your business, it is possible to add new services or products, or even to begin a second or third business.

You and your businesses will continue to grow and develop - so in selecting your first business idea, you are not saying 'no' to other opportunities. However, to give your first business idea a really strong start you might need to put other ideas on hold for a while, or at least on the back burner. Your current business model deserves your undivided attention at all times. Don't get distracted by the "shiny objects". By shiny objects, I mean the next big craze in the business world, the too good to be true niche, the next profitable venture or pyramid scheme. Don't do it. Be completely devoted to one idea at a time until it works or doesn't work.

THE INSPIRATION FOR YOUR NEW BUSINESS MAY COME FROM:

a. INVENTING SOMETHING NEW:

Some people are naturally good at finding original solutions to problems. Others come up with completely new ideas based on new technology or other developments. Sometimes people are driven to invent a solution when they are faced with a problem in their own life and realize there is no solution... yet.

b. TWEAKING SOMEONE ELSES IDEA TO MAKE IT BETTER:

This can be a great starting point. If an idea is working for one business, there's a good chance it could work for yours too. However, this one needs to be handled with care. If the marketplace is already overcrowded, you will need to offer something really special to earn your share of customers.

c. SPOTTING A GAP IN THE MARKET:

This often happens by accident. Perhaps you look everywhere for something you need, only to realize that no one in your area is providing it.

d. DEVELOPING YOUR OWN SKILLS AND INTERESTS:

Building on your own areas of expertise can be a great starting point, because you probably already understand the market and the needs of your potential customers quite well. Many people dream of earning a living doing something they love, and there is no reason why they shouldn't achieve this goal, given careful planning and hard work. Business ideas may be found in the most unexpected places or in everyday situations. Ideas don't need to be wildly inventive or original to succeed.

Ultimately your idea is only a good one if it allows you to create a sustainable business. It is important to assess your ideas objectively in the cold light of day. By all means, seek expert opinionsa and ask the opinions of people you trust. But make your own assessment of the facts as well. Business history is littered with examples of highly successful business ideas that no one but their inventor believed would work.

Thorough market research is critical - it can tell you whether customers really are willing to buy your product or service. It can also give you a good idea of what you should be charging and reveal who your competitors are.

Carrying out the following key steps will reveal whether you have a viable idea or not. At best they will give you a solid launch pad for your business; at worst they will reveal an unobtainable hurdle that causes you to seek out alternative ideas. But if there is a major problem, it is better to identify it now than six months down the line when you have already invested time, money and emotional energy into your idea.

CHAPTER FOUR

PICKING THE RIGHT NICHE WHEN STARTING YOUR OWN BUSINESS

One of the biggest mistakes you can make when starting your own business is picking the wrong niche. Picking the wrong niche can be detrimental to the success of your business and you may find it nearly impossible to make any money if you haven't done your research.

If you pick a niche that isn't hot you are setting yourself up for failure.

In picking the right niche:

a.   List all the skills you have.

b.   Think about the experiences you've gained in your work and personal life. List the most significant.

c.   List any other hobbies and interests you have.

d.   Ask your friends and family for their impressions of your greatest strengths and skills. Ask them to tell you honestly what they think your weakest points are in terms of setting up your own business.

e.   Look out for gaps in the market.

f.   Explore other businesses and identify those you might be able to build off of. Look for ways in which you can improve on the business in question. What can you offer that they do not? How can the product or service be improved?

Now, work through the following, and jot down your answer to each question:

a.   What is it that you will personally bring to the business in terms of relevant experience and expertise? In what way are you qualified to run this particular business?

b.   Just as importantly, are there any skills or is there any knowledge that you need to acquire before you can run this business?

c.   Is there a market - a need for the idea and customers who will pay for it?

d.   How big is the market, and how will you reach it?

e.   Who are your main competitors?

f.   How will you fund your business? (How much income do you need?)

g.   What might go wrong?

It will also help if you keep up-to-date with the current events to help you identify new trends and new products being launched.

ALSO, INVESTIGATE THE MARKETPLACE THOROUGHLY.

IDENTIFY YOUR CUSTOMERS AND GET TO KNOW THEIR LIKES AND DISLIKES.

Identify your competitors - how many of them are there, and how successful are they? Who is the lead player? Who is second? Find out as much as you can about them - collect brochures, marketing material and any other information you can. Test out their websites and call their customer service number or visit their shop or office if it is open to the public. Analyze their service or product honestly and objectively. What are their strengths? What are their weaknesses?

How much is it going to cost to launch your business (that is to get the first product on the shelf, to serve the first customer or to provide your service for your first client)?

WHERE IS THE MONEY GOING TO COME FROM?

Include money in your plan for contingencies. Consider what might go wrong - not just financially, but in other ways too such as legally, emotionally, physically. Plan for the unexpected and think through both the best and worst-case scenarios.

ASSESS YOUR BUSINESS'S LONG-TERM POTENTIAL.

Visualize yourself running your business. All this is necessary to pick the right niche.

CHAPTER FIVE

HOW TO FIND INVESTORS

Finding an investor for your business provides you with the seed money you may need to start the business. In return for investing in your business, most investors receive a percentage of the sales or company stock. Finding an investor for your business may be harder than it sounds, but there are a few ways to go about locating and convincing investors to invest in your business.

A good team of investors can play a great role in the success of your business, but a bad choice of investors can obliterate even the strongest ideas and business plans. Believe it or not, investors provide more opportunities to your business, while becoming resources for creating effective marketing ideas. Knowing what to consider while selecting investors and being able to attract the right type of investors are vital skills for established and emerging entrepreneurs. They want you to succeed just as much as you do, and often times offer more resources than just startup capital.

If you are a small business owner and finding trouble convincing investors, here are some secrets that will help you attract the eye of an angel investor or venture capital, while making your business a more appealing investment.

1.   GET THE MOST OUT OF NETWORKING

Networking is the best way for entrepreneurs to pitch their startup in a less formal and organic way. If you are building a great business, networking within the local startup and investing community can be the best way to meet and find the right type of investors. If you find investors interested in your business, keep the meetings going and let things happen organically for optimum results. Let them consider your business; after all, you are not only conveying your idea, you are actually relying on the social capital built through the networking process that impacts the investment decision.

2.   BE PRACTICAL, GET REAL PAYING CUSTOMERS

You need investment to attract customers, but you need customers to acquire money. It is always worth it to make an effort to get customers prior to approaching an investor, instead of seeking funds first and customers second. It is advised to create a plan to acquire customers first that doesn't need a very large investment.

This is very important, particularly for emerging entrepreneurs; it will become easier to get investors on good terms. Investors always want proof that your idea is effective enough and will work, and nothing will satisfy them than having real paying users.

3.   FIND THE RIGHT CO-FOUNDER

When you find investors, you are not only selling them your business in terms of products and services, you are selling them on your team. Opting for the right leadership team for your small business is an important process and having the wrong co-founders can be more dangerous for your business than having no co-founder at all. However, finding the right co-founder can make the process easier, even beyond attracting investors. As having partners will allow you to rely on them, which can be a huge boost for your startup.

4. GET A BETTER RETURN ON INVESTMENT (ROI)

Though investors may start believing in your business, the purpose of their investment is to make money. Therefore, it is important to highlight what they will actually gain from investing in your startup. No matter if you are approaching an angel, VC or a rich entrepreneur, it is important to show how you are going to obtain their investment return. It is alluring to focus on yourself and your business vision, but at the end of the day, investors want to know what is in it for them. Therefore, the best way to stand out and get interest is to clearly explain how and when they will see a return.

5. TAKE BENEFIT OF THE ONLINE FUNDRAISING MARKET

Networking is important, but your location should not be the restricting factor when it comes to securing an investment. There are different fundraising platforms available and you are no longer restricted to only being able to raise money. If your company has best-in-class metrics for your industry, you should be able to double your money. Post your business's best metrics and find investors on the platform related to your industry.

6. PICK THE RIGHT INVESTOR

In order to attract the attention of the right investor, make sure your product solves real problems. Many entrepreneurs only attempt to reinvent the wheel; therefore, it is advised to highlight the qualities of your product to attract the real investors. Doing so will get users and revenue. Think outside the box and do something useful.

7. GRADUATING FROM A TOP ACCELERATOR

Emerging and first-time entrepreneurs are advised to apply to reputable startup accelerators that will lead their credibility to your company. Joining an accelerator can be helpful for rising startups. Though it doesn't guarantee that you will attract investors, it does make your startup a more appealing investment candidate. Graduating from a reputable accelerator doesn't guarantee funding, but can greatly improve the chances that you would raise a favorable valuation.

8. WRITE A BUSINESS PLAN

Before looking for investors, write a business plan. A business plan is a written guide to your business including the purpose, the startup costs, expenses, sales forecasts and other information to gain the interest of investors.

9. MAKE A LIST OF POSSIBLE INVESTORS

Add people you know to the list who have money to invest and may be willing to take a risk with your business startup. Friends, family members and business owners of related businesses are the best places to start. For example, if your business involves a computer software product, then other software companies may be interested in investing in your company.

10. DEVELOP AN INVESTOR PRESENTATION

Compile a speech or pitch to present the business idea for convincing investors to invest in your startup. Include information in your presentation that includes what the product or service offering for the business is, the costs involved in starting the business, what kind of demand there is in the market for the product or service and how much the company stands to make in one year, three years and so on.

11.   CONTACT THE POSSIBLE INVESTORS

Schedule a time to meet with and make your presentation to each investor on your list.

12.   PRESENT YOUR BUSINESS IDEA TO INVESTORS

At the meeting with the investor(s), pitch your business by giving your presentation and providing a copy of your business plan. Answer any questions the investor has about the startup and tell the investor what is in for them such as shares of the company stock or a percentage of the sales. This is an interview; sell yourself and the company.

13.   SIGN AN INVESTOR AGREEMENT

Once you find an investor, put your agreement in writing. You can find general agreement templates online or work with a business attorney to help you draw up a legally binding contract for both you as the business owner and the investor to sign.

CHAPTER SIX

TAKE YOUR BUSINESS ONLINE, EVEN IF IT'S NOT INTERNET BASED

It is best for you to take advantage of what advanced technology has in store for you. The internet has opened for you a far wider access to more clients, distributors, and investors.

There are many of reasons why it is a good idea to take your business online, to name few:

1. ENHANCE BUSINESS CREDIBILITY

Nowadays, with the internet revolution, if your business does not exist online, it is more prone to losing credibility and competition in the market place.

2. ENHANCE PR

Having 24/7 access to important information about your business, contact info, product lists, etc... is a very powerful PR tool that your business can benefit from. Also, having free useful information for your clients' knowledge enrichment makes your website a valuable community resource; this means that more traffic will be driven to your website.

3. INCREASE PROFIT

Having more online traffic leads to more profit. Every year more and more people are making purchases online as opposed to walking into a store. It's easier, cheaper, and safer in terms of going to a store.

4. EVERYONE, EXCEPT YOU, IS DOING BUSINESS ONLINE

You've been left behind and that's why you feel that your business is not picking up. Before closing your doors or trying a new idea, try enlisting the help of a friend or a business partner on how to make your business online accessible. If not, you can surf the internet and find a company that will help you set up the system for an online business. These companies charge affordable prices in lieu for doing each and every detail for you.

5. YOU GET THE KNOWLEDGE ABOUT THE LATEST TECHNOLOGY

Sayng that the internet is the most effective medium by which people can get and process information is an understatement. For some people, it is the only right medium by virtue of the internet's speed and volume of materials for knowledge.

Being a business individual, you don't have any other tool that will help you succeed mores than the internet. From human resource management to incorporating new techniques in improving your operations and your product, the internet is ready to give you what you need.

6. YOU GET A WIDER ACCESS TO CLIENTS FROM BOTH IN-STORE AND ONLINE

You do not want to run a small business that doesn't allow you to come up with new products and services to offer. Online businesses can be accessed by more people all over the world. Everyone is doing their transactions online and you really have to accommodate the growing demand for products among people. If you cannot be accessed online, people will think that your business does not exist.

7. YOU SAVE TIME WHEN YOU TAKE YOUR BUSINESS ONLINE

Recent research findings have shown that people can save time and money as much as 60% percent of the time when transactions are done online. The Internet offers the fastest venue for communication among people apart from the faster mode of exchange of goods and services. For you, that is a way of finding time for you and your family.

8. Your money is safer when transactions are done online provided you take precautionary measures against scammers. Keep those passwords and important numbers in your head and do not share them with anybody. With an online business, there will be no checks to sign and no cash to take to the bank.

9. GET MORE SATISFIED CUSTOMERS

An online presence will allow you to provide your customers or prospects with immediate answers to their questions without them waiting for your physical storefront to open, being placed on hold, or awaiting delivery of your company brochure. Saving your customers time, in turn, saves you the exorbitant cost of print advertising design, manufacture and mailing - and possibly the cost of losing your prospect during the wait.

10. REDUCE OPERATING COSTS

You can sell your products and services online and automate responses to customers without the need for additional sales or customer service staff.

11. MINIMAL INVESTMENT, HIGHER RETURNS

Whether you build your website yourself, purchase a low-cost template or get a custom design by a professional designer, a successful website produces a higher return on investment than any other medium. Consider the cost of a website compared to the expense of an ad in the Yellow Pages (that nobody reads anyways), print marketing materials or the additional staff required to offer round-the-clock service, and you'll find that a website can offer your business greater exposure, savings and profit potential than other methods for only a fraction of the price.

Taking your business online and promoting it regularly may dramatically increase your sales and get you ready for other big plans and promotions. It's a great way to encourage and engage your customers. Now the question is, when are you going to take your business online?

BUILD A BRAND

Small businesses get started in a variety of ways. Most small businesses have gone through the rigor of developing a business plan. However, the really successful small businesses also think about how to build a brand, not just a business. Your brand communicates who you are and what you do as a business. It helps you stand out from competitors in your market. It represents a promise to your customers that when they buy your product or service, they will receive a certain value every time.

When most people think of branding, they think of logos, taglines, value propositions, advertising slogans, and other common branding tools. But there's a lot of different ways to build a brand.

TO BUILD BRAND:

1. BUILD A BRAND WITH DISTINCTION

It is critical to be distinctive if you want to build a brand. Let's be honest and admit that few small businesses offer something that no one ever thought of before. So, how do you make yourself attractive to your customers? You must create a distinct and engaging brand personality. Your brand should be the person your customer wants to do business with.

You want to be memorable and stand for something. You must be distinctive enough that you can build a brand. Otherwise, you will just be another supplier in the category.

2. BUILD A BRAND WITH CONSISTENCY

Once you've created this distinct brand personality, you must be consistent. The only way to build a brand is to stay with the message. Small businesses frequently chase everything that gets in front of them. Avoid the tendency to become reactionary. Stay true to your message with your personality. It is the repetition and consistency that will build a brand for you.

Small business owners frequently get tired of their own brand long before the customer does. Just because you are bored with something doesn't mean it isn't working or that your customers are bored too. You live with your brand everyday, your customers probably don't. So don't fall into the trap of change for the sake of change. If you want to build a strong brand it will take time.

3. BUILD A BRAND BY EVOLVING

There will be times when you need to change. Make certain that you evolve the brand. Listen to your customers. Their perception of your brand is your reality. Keep the brand fresh and relevant but true to your original core values. After all, those values are what made you stand out in the first place.

Don't lose that. Evolution is part of building a brand.

4. BUILD A BRAND WITH GUTS

To build a brand you must also embrace it. Don't be afraid of what it is. Don't pull your punches. Sometimes to be true to the brand you built you might not be attractive to another part of the marketplace. If you water your brand down so that it includes everyone, you probably don't stand for anything. Don't water down your niche and become too broad. You can't please everyone.

ALSO, BUILD YOUR BRAND WITH:

6. INTERIOR DESIGN: The way your place of business looks on the inside sends a powerful message about your commitment to the business. Is your interior neat, clean, and professional? This goes the same for online websites as well.

Does it make clients feel welcome when they walk through the door? Does it reflect the look and feel that clients expect from your type of business? Investing in interior design shows that you are serious about the business and plan to be around for a long time. By itself, the interior design probably won't cause a prospect to do business with you. However, it can definitely swing their decision in the right (or wrong) direction.

7.   PERSONAL BRANDING: As head of the business, you are your company's leading brand ambassador. Which means everything you think, do and say contributes to your brand. The way you dress, your posture, the way you speak - these all play a role in shaping customers' perceptions about the value of doing business with you. There are many ways to develop your personal brand, but the key is to make sure it aligns with your company's brand. If you're selling tailored suits, you had better look like a million bucks.

8.   PARTIES AND SOCIAL EVENTS: As a business owner, you're on even when you're off. At non-work parties and social events, you're still representing your business. This gives you an excellent opportunity to build your brand. Parties allow you to meet new people, reconnect with those you already know, and identify people who could be clients, strategic partners or referral sources. Hosting a party or event doubles the opportunity, as it obligates you to interact with all the guests.

9.   YOUR CAR: Your business may not lend itself to such a campy look or humorous approach. But with a little ingenuity, your car may help to build your brand every time you drive it.

10.   YOUTUBE VIDEOS: Creating your own YouTube channel and videos offers an inexpensive and very effective way to build your brand. Videos can include everything from "verbal" white papers to customer testimonials, industry thought leadership and more. Today's viewers expect videos with high production quality, so don't post anything that looks sloppy, cheap, or homemade.

Everything you do as a business contributes to your brand - the purpose of which is to define, differentiate and communicate your unique value proposition. Never try to imitate another brand. Instead, get creative about your own brand, and build your brand communications around what will hit home with your customers or clients. So go ahead and be who you are.

If you've done your homework you will have your audience. Others will find you attractive because you stick to your core values. It's okay if some people don't like who you are as a brand. That means you stand for something. Again, you can't please everyone.

CHAPTER SEVEN

COMMON MISTAKES MADE BY NEW BUSINESS OWNERS

Most new small businesses won't be in business this time next year. That's the cold hard truth behind it. Though it is easy to start your own business, it takes a lot more to succeed in business. There are common mistakes made by small business owners. Let's explore them so you can avoid them.

1. NEGLECTING YOUR CONTINUING EDUCATION

You are the only renewable resource, besides your employees, your business has. You may be a master at getting the most out of your other resources, but how are you doing with you?

Today's world is characterized by rapid change. Keeping up on innovations in your business and new business strategies is crucial for long-term success. However, most small business owners do not invest any time or money into developing themselves. The less you know, the more time, money and energy you will waste employing others who do.

2. UNREALISTIC EXPECTATIONS

There's an old saying in business that says you can have things fast, good, or affordable. It goes on to state that the best you can usually do is two out of three so decide which two are most important to you and go forward from there. Fast and affordable may not be good, and fast and good will probably cost you more than you'd like to pay. Expecting all three each and every time may be, well, unrealistic.

3. FAILING TO PLAN IS PLANNING TO FAIL

Many small business owners avoid planning at all costs. The old adage, "Failing to plan is planning to fail", is true. Without a well-thought out plan for establishing your business, running your business, and marketing your business, you will waste a lot of time. The time you don't have.

So, how do we find time to plan while we're trying to run a business? Do the work in small increments. Keep a notebook handy throughout your day. Have sections designated for "Operations", "Finance", and "Marketing". Make notes as random thoughts appear to you during the day. At the end of each week, take an hour or so and summarize the ideas into a plan. Place the actions that will yield the highest potential return at the top of the list. Start Monday of the next week by tackling the items at the top of your list.

4. ALL WORK AND NO PLAY

Running your own business is hard work. There is no doubt about that. However, without proper relaxation, you will become increasingly less productive. It isn't the hours you spend at work but the productivity of the hours you spend there. Become a student of your own business. When do most customers access your business? When is the slow time of the day or week? If you are available for an entire hour that may only yield one small sale, you may be better off out of the office.

Take a walk. Talk to people along the way. They could be future customers. Join a gym and work out during half of that slow hour. This kills two birds with one stone. You become healthier with better endurance and again, you can network with people who might be future customers.

5. TAKE YOUR EXISTING CUSTOMERS FOR GRANTED

Remember the first customer you ever had? Remember the appreciation you had for them? Remember the little things you did for them? When did you stop and WHY?

Avoid looking after your existing customers and they will go elsewhere. Customers have more options today than they ever had before. If they don't find your competitor locally, they will find them on the Internet. Ignore customers at your own expense.

The fact is without them you wouldn't be in business. It's time to make certain they understand how much you really appreciate them. How about having a special reception or buffet on site for your customers? What about a special appreciation day?

When was the last time you contacted customers just to tell them how much you appreciate their business? A happy customer is a valuable business asset, now and in the future.

6. NEVER ASK FOR REFERRALS

As stated above, your existing, happy customers are a major business asset. That asset can yield benefits in many ways. But you have to ask. Instead of spending a lot of money on your advertising, why not ask customers for referrals? Referral sales are the cheapest and easiest way to grow your business.

7. ONE-STOP SHOP MENTALITY

Many business owners fail to achieve their true potential because they try to be all things to all people. You need to target your ideal customers. Look at your product. Ask yourself who would benefit most from your product. Once you have selected a targeted group, learn everything you can about them.

Change your store or website to reflect that targeted customer's needs and desires. Speak their language. Find out where they hang out and what they read or listen to. Understand their concerns. Sell them solutions, not products, and you will excel!

8. NEGLECTING MARKETING

It is so easy for a business owner to get caught up in the daily operations of a business. The inventory ordering, order processing, data input, hiring and more, can become all-consuming. Then one day you look up and wonder what happened to the business.

Marketing is all about future sales. You plant the seed today to reap the benefits tomorrow. If you want a long-term successful business you can hand off to your children or sell for retirement, don't neglect marketing. Every month, set aside at least 20% of your time dedicated to marketing activities.

Marketing activities include deciding to expand an existing product line, dumping unprofitable products or adding new products. Determine where your advertising can generate the biggest return on the investment and plan out your marketing process. These are crucial functions for your success. Again, neglect them at your own expense!

9. THINKING YOU DON'T NEED A BUSINESS PLAN

Yes, you do! Business plans force you to examine your concept, study the competition, think about costs and plan a long-term winning strategy. A business plan is most often used to seek start-up funding, proving to the lender that the business will succeed. Even if you don't need funding, taking the time to plan your business before running it is the smartest step you can make towards long-term success.

10.   MENTAL BOOKKEEPING

Keeping "the books" all in your head is a great way to get into big financial trouble. Expenses and income need to be carefully documented. Suppliers, customers, and the IRS aren't going to accept "oh, it was about $3500, give or take" when they come to you looking for a receipt.

There are many different ways to keep your books. If you prefer not to track of your finances with pencil and paper, try one of the many bookkeeping software packages available. If you still feel that you can't keep on top of making timely entries, hire a bookkeeper or accountant to keep all your business finances in order. You will be glad you did.

11.   SPENDING MONEY YOU DIDN'T NEED TO SPEND

Don't blow through all your startup capital. If you've done your business plan as you should, you will understand your break-even point. Budget carefully so that your business can operate beyond that point. Expect the unexpected and be prepared for sudden market changes, late-paying customers or other unforeseen expenses beyond your control. Don't fall into the trap of buying into the latest fad or gimmick before thoroughly checking it out.

12.   LACK OF BALANCE

While starting and running your own business requires a lot of hard work and dedication, ignoring loved ones can be as detrimental to your emotional and physical health as the business failing.

Make sure that family and close companions understand and accept that you'll be working long hours to get your dream off the ground. By the same token, make sure that you don't abandon them. There are some life experiences that are not repeatable. Take the time off to enjoy them.

13.   COMMON MISCONCEPTIONS

You just need a great idea or technology. There is no such thing as the "perfect idea" – only how you implement it. Everyone has great ideas, the trick is to tap into a market need and create a winning product or service that solves a problem or a need. Many ventures hire their technical talent; the leader has a vision of the market that leads to success. You understand the market because you have talked to a few friends. Thorough market research is required to know who will buy, and why, to determine what characteristics will cause your product or service to appeal. If you can't answer, "what problem does this solve", then you don't have a viable business idea. You have no competitors. All businesses have competitors because anyone can choose to spend their money on something else, even if it isn't the same as what you are doing or developing.

14.   NOT PLANNING FOR GROWTH

All entrepreneurs want to grow their business. They want to be in a situation where progressive steps toward becoming a larger organization happen daily. Often though, many small business IT systems were not purchased with the intention or potential for growth. This can be for a variety of reasons, lack of knowledge, budgetary limitations, or even failure to plan effectively. No matter the reason, the lack of scalability can lead to a very cost ineffective repeat purchasing of technology.

15.   NO PLAN FOR SOCIAL MEDIA MARKETING

There is currently a huge buzz about the business benefits of social media. So much so that business owners rushed to get online and have their websites optimized for search engines several years ago. Businesses all over the world are frantically trying to establish a presence on sites like Twitter, Facebook, Google Plus and LinkedIn. Countless businesses have figured out how best to use these sites and are already reaping massive rewards.

However, many are floundering too because they tend to make certain types of mistakes.

Sadly, many business owers are seduced by the numbers. They end up buying fans and followers. Doing so is a complete waste of money. If you are in business and new to social media, it helps a lot if you can avoid making these common mistakes. The key is to log into these sites regularly and be active on them. Engage with others often. Ask compelling questions, and offer thoughtful answers. Share, retweet, and like often. Always be friendly, helpful and polite. Slowly but surely your business will make an impact, and the benefits will accumulate.

Staying focused upon these common business mistakes can save you a lot of time and money. They are also crucial to the ongoing success of your business. Stay focused on the future while you work in the present. Don't develop work habits counterproductive to a successful outcome.

CONCLUSION

Now is the best time to start a business, launch a product or offer a cutting edge new service. More people than ever have jobs. More people than ever own homes. More business organizations are established each year than the previous year. Global prosperity is galloping along, with formerly poor countries seeing spectacular growth (potential new customers for new products and services) in the middle class.

The opportunity to successfully start a business, market an invention or new service is always dependent solely on the value, novelty, and benefits of the new offering. If there is an under-served market segment and you can identify a niche in a large market category, the time is always right to move ahead.

Time is never an entrepreneur's friend. Do not delay movement to commercialize an opportunity based on short-term business conditions, perceived or real. For example, interest rates have been historically low for the last several years. Recently they have begun to inch up. How high will they go? What effect might the rise have on the ultimate success for your venture? No one really knows the exact answer. We only can state with certainty that rates go up, rates go down. Look at the historic averages and anticipate that these averages will hold true to form. Base your financial assumptions on the mean averages, but do not delay movement on a great idea because of uncertainty about one element. Remember, if lending rates go up, they rise for your competition as well.

Also, do not listen to negative nannies nit picking your project. If you have done an effective job of due-diligence, can identify your market niche as being under-served and can quantify an excellent financial proposition, you probably have the makings of a successful business. You will certainly know more than the critics. It is easier for people to be negative than to encourage your interest in taking a risk to start your own business. Risk equates to possible failure for most people. You will be changing your life and most people instinctively fear change.

Seek advice from friends, family and valued independent counselors. It is important to know as much about your project's strengths and weaknesses as possible before committing your energy and resources.

Also know that successful entrepreneurs almost always have an inner compass which sorts through the mass of concerns, objections, and negatives they receive. It is always easier to say no and not move forward than to commit and push ahead.

America is teeming with dreamers and doers, all hoping to succeed in a cluttered, very aggressive marketplace. Delay is never a wise course of non-action if your project has real legs and commercial viability. Somebody else is potentially working on a spot on a competitive product. You cannot afford to lose your market advantage because of dallying and uncertainty about entering the market at the optimum time. There is never a perfect time to start. There is only now and now is plenty good enough. If you have a great idea and don't pursue it, I promise you will end up kicking yourself in the future for not giving it a shot. You will never know until you try.

So, what are you waiting for? Start your own business NOW and turn your dreams into a reality!

Keep reading for a sneak peek into the next book released by K. Connors!

FLIPPING HOUSES

The Complete Guide on How to Buy, Sell and Invest in Real Estate

By K. Connors

TABLE OF CONTENT

INTRODUCTION

Flipping houses is one of the best ways to make money when it comes to real estate investing. Approximately 90% of the world's millionaires made their money through some sort of real estate investing. But how can an ordinary person flip houses and make a substantial amount of money in today's real estate market? What are the main things you need to understand before going and flipping a house? And why is it important to educate yourself before flipping a house? In this book, I will go over key topics that will assist you in your house flipping venture.

If you want to maximize profits with real estate investing, then flipping houses is definitely an avenue to pursue. Flipping properties is a term that is typically used in real estate; it is when an investor takes control of a property and quickly resells it for a profit. Some flippers will also perform renovations; however, this can be risky and isn't recommended for the novice investor. The process starts by finding a home to flip. The property should be under priced for the current local market. Often times these properties are called 'fixer uppers', but not all the time. Any foreclosure, pre-foreclosure, auction, or home that has been neglected can be bought for a lower price. Flipping properties is commonly done by dealers or retailers, but it is more than possible for anyone to take part in the art of flipping properties.

After you have found a suitable property, you will typically purchase the property. However, there are other ways to control the property for as little as a few bucks. These transactions leave the flipper with control of the property, but without the normal burden of having to worry about the mortgage payments. Once in control of a property, it becomes the flippers job to market it to potential buyers. The marketing process can involve anything from local marketing through newspaper ads and standard signage to building a relationship with one or multiple local realtors. There are also more advanced methods such as internet marketing. Your goal is to get the property seen by as many people as possible, and as quick as possible. Time is money, so the more potential buyers that are exposed to the property the better.

Once the property has been sold, the flipper should then immediately begin looking for their next property. It is not uncommon for more experienced flippers to control five to seven properties at any given time.

CHAPTER 1

WHAT IS HOUSE FLIPPING?
Flipping houses is a great way to earn money in real estate. You buy a property, fix it (or don't) and then sell it for a profit. These three things are the primary principles of house flipping where an investor can earn substantial profits. An investor that is able to buy, fix and then sell a house quickly emerges with money and profits that they can use to fund their next real estate investment.

BUYING A PROPERTY

This is the very first thing you need to do in order to get started in flipping houses. Consider, however, the funding that you will need to purchase a property. Do you have the cash to buy the property? Will you be applying for a bank loan? Do you have a partner with whom you can share the costs of purchasing the house? Depending on your financial situation, financing, and funding, these are important things to consider before buying a house to be flipped. In buying a house, it is important to consider the location and the structural quality of the property. Choose a house in a decent neighborhood so that the property will be easy to sell later on. Determine as well the improvements that are necessary. Check for leaks as well as damaged flooring, plumbing, and roofing. Try to assess if the house you are considering is well worth your effort. Usually, experienced house flippers choose properties wherein minor repairs are necessary, such as installing new carpeting, cabinets, repainting, and gardening.

Your goal is to make money so it is ideal to buy a property that's priced below market value. Finding motivated sellers is one way to buy a low-priced house. These motivated sellers are people who wish to sell their houses for fast cash. Job relocation, divorce or death in the family may oblige people to sell their homes at considerably low prices.

Distressed properties are also low-priced homes that you can look into. Look for announcements of foreclosures in the newspaper and see if you can bid for the property. However, be very careful as some foreclosed properties don't offer a preview of the house; thus, giving you no clue of its marketability.

Buying a house to be flipped involves several factors which include location, price, and structural value. Start by buying a property for the average American family. This is usually a house with three bedrooms, two bathrooms, a living room, kitchen, dining room, garage and a beautiful outdoor area.

FIX THE HOUSE

Renovations and improvements are the next step that you should do in flipping houses. Set a budget for the materials, labor and overall expenses that you need to make. Determine whether you'd like to hire a contractor for the job or do the fixing yourself. Try to find the cheapest labor, if at all possible. You, an older son and college kids who need money can do all the fixing. Apart from setting a budget, you also need to have a timeframe for the project. Time is of the essence in house flipping as a house that sits too long in the market, is no longer profitable. Usually, a house must be sold within 90 days from the time of purchase.

In fixing a house, focus on key aspects that can boost the value of the property. A well-tended lawn is one as well as replacing broken electrical wires and plumbing fixtures. Make a detailed outline of the materials and items that you will need for the entire project. Keep the design of the house simple and clean, yet attractive.

SELL THE HOUSE

Everything boils down to eventually selling the house for a profit when it comes to investing in real estate. Stage an open house and invite people to come and see the home. Market the event and inform as many people as possible about it. You can even prepare and send out flyers to your friends. Write a press release about the house and talk about the property in social networking sites and forums. Use descriptive words and phrases when telling people about the property. Instead of merely saying "house for sale," write "modern opulence" or "Twilight cottage." Do your best to sell the property as fast as you can. Flipping houses can be a very lucrative full time and even part time job if done properly.

This may just be what you need to do in order to earn more money. Invest in house flipping projects and enter the world where huge profits can be generated in a short amount of time.

HOUSE FLIPPING; CAN YOU STILL MAKE MONEY?

By now you already know that buying run down properties, fixing them up, and selling them for a profit is known as 'house flipping'. Not just from me, but due to the glut of TV shows that focus on this method of real estate investing. However, the housing market has definitely changed over the past few years or so. Prices in most areas of the US have stabilized, and in some areas, they have fallen. Can a house flipper still be successful in an environment like this?

Yes, it's still possible and even probable to make a lot of money, even in a stagnant market. However, the average investor needs to be a lot more careful nowadays. In the previous gung-ho housing market, most flippers could count on market appreciation to save them even if they had numerous unexpected costs and delays. The fact that it was a seller's market would more often than not ensure that they at least broke even, and in some cases, scored unexpectedly high profits. To be perfectly honest, this isn't all too likely to happen with current conditions. Finding the right property to start with is now paramount. Many experienced flippers were saying all along that the profit is made when the house is bought, not when it's sold, and now this is truer than ever.

The problem is compounded by the fact that the media popularity of house flipping has brought a lot of new investors into the market, making competition for suitable houses more intense. In some markets, mostly high-priced ones, bidding wars are occurring for fixer-uppers, due to interest both from investors, and from individuals who want to buy a house to live in but have been priced out of the market. In these areas, finding a property that will allow a profit after the costs of renovating and marketing are figured in can be like finding a needle in a haystack.

However, if you live near or look in areas where prices are more moderate, making money with flipping is still possible. You do have to be careful about sticking to some tried-and-tested rules, however.

First of all, make sure your projected improvements will not require you to set a sale price that's out of line with the neighborhood. If you buy the worst house on the block for $150,000 and comparable homes in good condition go for around $190,000, don't set a budget of $40,000. It's a fact that you'll wind up going over budget more often than not. Even if you do manage to hold the line, you'll still need to ask at least $220,000 to break even after allowing for realtor fees, carrying costs, and the other little expenses that add up.

In this market, trying to sell for that much over the norm may mean a long wait. It's much easier to set a budget of $20,000 and make the house presentable, which will more than likely result in a much quicker sale.

Another thing that can affect the end result is the renovation timeline. If you plan to complete the renovation in four weeks and it winds up taking twelve, you'll have at least two additional mortgage payments. Depending on how much those payments are, this delay could remove any potential for profit. At the least, it surely makes it more difficult.

Something else to keep in mind is to remember that you're not renovating the house to live in but to sell. Therefore, make sure the renovations appeal to the great majority of possible buyers, not just to your own tastes. Ignoring this rule was something that many flippers, including myself got away with during the boom market. However, in tighter financial times, purchasers paying a premium for a totally redone property will prefer to get exactly that - not something they need to redecorate.

Lastly, once the house is finished, stage it. As you may know, staging refers to the furnishing of the house and making it look lived in. Some studies have shown that staging can cause a property to sell 40% faster. The process of staging will not only attract more buyers, but will also frequently get a larger number of realtors involved. Also, don't forget the outside when staging. Improving curb appeal by arranging to landscape in an attractive manner will make a big difference in how many prospective buyers actually make it through the front door. Lots of people will just drive away if they don't like the exterior of a house. So, if you're up for the challenge, you can still make a lot of money flipping houses. Just realize that now you can't count on the contribution of that silent partner called market appreciation, unless you're in a highly valued area, in which case your buying prices will be extraordinarily higher.

CHAPTER 2

GETTING STARTED WITH REFERRALS

It seems that everywhere you turn these days, there is so much hype and buzz about investing in real estate. You can't even flip through your TV channels without encountering a show telling you to "Flip This House," or "Flip That House." To someone who is just learning about real estate investing, all of this can seem rather intimidating. So, I'll try to get you going with the absolute easiest way to get into flipping houses, and that is through referrals. This simply means that you will be referring deals to other investors and get paid to do so. To get started with referrals, you don't even need money or skill. All you need is a little knowledge and the right direction.

There are many ways to approach referrals for house flipping, but I'd like to outline a very simple plan for you to get started:

- Identify properties that may have a motivated seller.

- Obtain a minimal amount of qualifying information.

- Pass this information on to an experienced investor that you trust.

- Discuss compensation with the experienced investor that you're working with.

- Evaluate and make adjustments, based on each experienced investor, you work with.

1. IDENTIFY PROPERTIES THAT MAY HAVE A MOTIVATED SELLER

Almost all real estate deals start out with someone who needs to sell, in which selling quickly can be more important than the profit motive. It doesn't mean that they don't have a profit motive, it just means that they would rather sell sooner, than wait until later to get top dollar. Some examples of properties that may have a motivated seller are: fire damaged properties, houses that are vacant, houses that are in serious disrepair, neglected, have high grass, aren't getting the snow shoveled in the winter time, have mail stacking up, etc.

2. OBTAIN A MINIMAL AMOUNT OF QUALIFYING INFORMATION

This is where a lot of people get burned out before they ever get started. In the referral business, you are learning the basics of "how to flip a house," you are not actually flipping houses. Therefore, you should not be working as hard as someone who is actually flipping houses. Let's say you are driving around one day, looking for houses, one that has been seriously neglected and is in desperate need of expensive exterior repairs (i.e. The house is "ugly"). In the house flipping business, this is a technique we call "driving for dollars." It doesn't take long before you find a vacant, ugly house.

So what information should you get? Obviously, you will need the address. It would also be a great idea to use a digital camera or cell phone to take a picture of at least the front of the house, but preferably the front and back. Remember, I don't want you to work too hard yet, so I don't even want you to get out of your car to take these pictures if you don't have to. You will email the photos when you contact the investor.

3. PASS THIS INFORMATION ON TO AN EXPERIENCED INVESTOR THAT YOU TRUST

Now you should already have, or should immediately build a list of 10-20 investors you can call on the phone, or send an email to, or contact through their websites. You will put this list together from the following sources: Real Estate Investment Clubs, Newspapers, Ads and street signs from people advertising "We Buy Houses," and maybe even some "For Rent" signs from the same neighborhood that you found the vacant, ugly house. Contact several of these investors and find at least one that you trust. Try them out on some of your referrals. If it doesn't work out, simply move on to the next property on your list. Only work with one at a time, because you may not be experienced or skilled enough to protect yourself with contracts yet. Therefore, working with too many people is just inviting someone to "steal your deal" without compensating you for it.

4. DISCUSS COMPENSATION WITH THE INVESTOR THAT YOU'RE WORKING WITH

Realize that you will only get paid if and when the investor you referred the deal to actually buys the property. Since you are just starting out, ask for and expect to receive, a fee between $100-$250 for the information and photos you are providing. Remember how I told you that I didn't want you to work that hard right? If you can get paid $100 for just making a phone call or sending an email, believe me, it's worth it! "But who the heck is going to pay this kind of money for a few lousy pictures?" Many, many investors who own multiple properties and buy monthly will be more than happy to spend a couple hundred dollars for some information they don't have time to gather themselves. Believe me, I did this for about 8 months before I even made an offer on my first home. You aren't just doing it for the money, but for the knowledge and the experience you will undoubtedly gain in the process.

5. EVALUATE AND MAKE ADJUSTMENTS, BASED ON EACH EXPERIENCED INVESTOR YOU WORK WITH

As you refer each deal to one or more investors, you will get a feel for what they are looking for. If you start out working with one investor and he or she is only looking for 3-bedroom, brick houses on the north side of town, you can also start working with another investor who may be looking for 2-bedroom duplexes on the north side of town.

Many "would-be investors" get burned out before they ever get started in-house flipping because they try to figure out what all the investors in their city want before they even do anything. Then, they try to provide too much information, and aren't happy with their compensation. I want you to do minimal work at first, while making a maximum dollar for the amount of time you are involved. Now, try out what you've learned here, and let me know how it's working!

CHAPTER 3

MYTHS ON HOUSE FLIPPING

Many investors dive into the world of house flipping not just because of profitable margins, but also because it is a very enjoyable endeavor. However, one must be careful before entering this realm because not all available information is true. Some are myths that may sound true because they are popularized. This chapter involves debunking some of the top myths associated with house flipping.

A. YOU CAN'T FLIP A HOUSE WHEN YOU DON'T HAVE ADEQUATE MONEY

The common idea among newbies is that house flipping can't be done when you don't have sufficient money of your own. This belief is absolutely incorrect because house flipping can be a partnership. You and other people can pool your money together to flip a house. Perhaps, you can have personal loans from other family members and friends, and use the amount collected to flip the house you want. Money is all around you.

B. YOU CAN'T FLIP A HOUSE WHEN YOU ARE NOT A HANDY MAN

House flipping requires renovation, fixes, and rehabilitation tasks. However, it does not require you to be hands on with all of these. Some tasks can be done on your own to reduce costs, but it is still not a prerequisite for a total house flipping income. Even the experienced house flippers tap into the services of house renovation teams not only to reduce the effort, but also because of the professional expertise imparted by these skilled workers. The pros can accomplish the tasks in a shorter time frame. This translates to more money added to your savings.

Remember that house flipping entails renovating and fixing flaws of a purchased house to make it more conducive for living. There is no model house for this because all homes can be flipped and sold. However, it can certainly help if you are able to scout homes that have strong foundations and those that may require few fixes.

C. FLIPPING A HOUSE REQUIRES YOU TO SELL IT

While it is the general idea of house flipping, there are many things that could happen during and after the renovation stages. One such thing is the possibility that the flipped house would stay in the selling market for too long. When this happens, the investor can resort to have the property available for rent. After the renovation tasks, the house flipper can also fall in love with the flipped house and live in it themselves.

More than flipping and selling a house, an investor can also flip and rent, and flip and leave.

CHAPTER 4

CREATING YOUR BUSINESS PLAN
The house flipping process can be divided into three phases: home buying, home renovating, and home selling. Each phase is important and challenging and each phase will build off of the successes and failures of the previous phases.

1. HOME BUYING

This phase is the most critical phase because it will set the tone for the rest of your house flipping project. If you select the wrong house to flip, you will be forced to pay higher than expected construction costs and forced to deal with a longer than the anticipated selling period. On the flip side (pun intended), if you choose the right house, the construction and selling process will virtually take care of themselves. Most real estate experts will agree that you do not make money with the sale of your flipped houses, but with the purchase of the house, as mentioned before. You always want to have the end goal in mind. The end goal in house flipping is obviously to make money. Therefore, selecting the right house to fit your budget and your schedule makes for an easy time renovating and selling the house.

2. HOME RENOVATION

The best strategy to follow to ensure a successful house flip is to set your budget and your schedule before you begin construction. With a budget and schedule set, you will know how much money you can spend for your flip as well as how long the flip will take. This way you can better track your progress. In construction, the three most important factors to produce a final product are time, money and quality. All three of these factors are interrelated. For example, if you want to speed up the construction process, it is going to cost you more money and the quality of the work will be affected, most likely negatively. If you are looking to install the finest quality features in your house, it will probably cost you more time and more money. Finally, if want to spend the least amount of money as possible, expect the quality to suffer and the duration of the project to last longer. The goal here is to find a happy medium where none of the above factors are drastically affected.

3. HOME SELLING

Depending on how well you researched your target market and what type of improvements you've added to your flip in the previous phases, the home selling phase should only last a few weeks. Anything longer than a month and you will be forced to pay an additional mortgage payment which will reduce your overall profits. To make sure that you sell the flipped house quickly, I would advise that you follow these two guides: set your selling price below or right at the market value and market your home.

The name of the game in house flipping is speed and when you set the selling price of your house below or right at the market average, potential home buyers will see the added benefits of your renovation in conjunction with your lower asking price and immediately see a tremendous value. Is this possible even with renovation costs? You bet it is.

Also, the more potential home buyers you can have looking at your house, the more likely someone will like and ultimately buy your flipped home. There is no one right way to flip a house. However, some ways are significantly better than others. What works for some projects may not work for others. Determine your budget and schedule and always have an end goal in mind straight from the beginning. If you can successfully do that, you are well on your way to a successful house flipping project.

WHAT YOU NEED TO INCLUDE IN YOUR BUDGET FOR HOUSE FLIPPING

Many people are enticed into house flipping by television images of people ripping materials out of a dilapidated house, refurbishing it, and selling it for a substantial profit. The profit realized from each flip can be modest or substantial - or the investor could lose everything depending on decisions made before or during the process. I'm not here to sugar coat anything, as this is the realty of investing in real estate. This is what separates the successful investors from the amateurs.

HOUSE FLIPPING BUDGET CHECKLIST

Before you go shopping for the perfect rehab-to-flip property, you need to create a budget for the entire project, not just the purchase and rehab expenses. The first item on your checklist does not have a direct monetary value and cannot be added in the expenses column. However, it is an important "ingredient" to your budget: an excellent credit score. Unless you are funding a flip entirely with cash or through private means, an excellent credit score works in your favor with the banks; especially when the loan is a high-risk project like a house flip.

NOW, LET'S LOOK AT THE SPECIFICS OF YOUR BUDGET

A. THE AFTER REPAIR VALUE (ARV): Determining the ARV of your potential flip is the starting point on which you can base your expected return on investment (ROI) when the house is put on the market. A trusted realtor can help you estimate the ARV of the property.

B. REHAB COSTS: These will vary widely depending on how much rehab work needs to be done. A budget repair form can be handy for tracking all the repairs needed.

C. FINANCING/CARRYING COSTS: These include not only the loan, but also the costs of carrying the house until it is sold:

- Financing loan(s)

- Property taxes

- Utilities (gas, water, electric)

- Property insurance

- HOA/Condo fees

80

An important point to note here is that the longer the rehab work takes and/or the longer the post-rehab house stays on the market, the greater you're carrying costs and the lesser profit you may realize.

D. REALTOR'S FEES: you can sell your flipped house yourself (FSOB - For Sale by Owner), but if you are looking for the fastest turnaround on your investment - and profit - relying on a good real estate agent is worth the commission fee (and actually helps you save money on your flip project in the long run).

E. FORGOTTEN COSTS: these are additional expenses of house flipping that are often overlooked, including:

- Inspection fees

- Interest on loans

- Contingencies

- Closing costs

An average house flipper's average budget can be broken down into roughly these cost percentages:

- 53.25% = Purchase Price

- 20% = Labor

- 6.5% = Materials

- 8% = Carrying costs, utilities, commissions, etc.

- 12.25% = Profit

Realistic budgeting = reduced risk

There is nothing that can completely eliminate the risks inherent in house flipping, but creating a realistic budget is one of the key ways to mitigate some of that risk. Another way to "manage" some of the risks is to become as thoroughly knowledgeable about house flipping before you make your first investment. A final way to manage risk is to follow the old saying "never invest more than you can afford to lose".

BASIC HOUSE FLIPPING AND WHOLESALING COSTS

When starting a wholesaling business, there can be substantial wholesaling and house flipping costs. Not only will you be in charge of finding leads, finding the buyers, bringing them together, working with the title company and even dealing with contracts, you'll also be covering the costs until and when that house sells. No one wants to muck-up the process to worry about unpaid bills and trying to finance these wholesaling efforts. Yet, it comes with the territory. Luckily, most of these costs come at closing and can be paid for by the buyer. When they aren't though, you can be prepared for them by knowing about those costs ahead of time.

When involved in wholesaling there are two levels of cost. The first is the cost associated with house flipping. The second is the cost associated with wholesaling. These are two separate, but closely related enterprises.

BASIC HOUSE FLIPPING COSTS

House flippers earn money via purchasing the flip first, fixing it up and placing it with a real estate agent to try and sell the property for top dollar. As an investor your house flipping costs will be similar to that of the expenses associated when purchasing a home to live in or selling it:

1. REALTOR FEES

When the house actually sells on the market, you'll probably have a realtor's commission to pay. However, this usually comes out of the profits from the sale of the real estate property. This is usually no more than about 6% of the selling price. When turning over multiple homes, you can negotiate lower fees.

2. CARRYING COSTS

These are the basic costs of owning a home. You won't have to worry about them when starting a wholesaling business, but if you intend to be a house flipper this is what you'll be responsible for:

- Property Taxes

- Regular Maintenance

- Electric, Gas, Etc.

- Mortgage

The longer you hold that property in your name, the more house flipping costs you'll have. The more cost you have, the less your profit will be.

3. LOAN COSTS

House flippers can also buy the house they intend to flip using credit. This can mean a mortgage in your name if you don't use cash out of pocket that you'll have to make back on the sale of the property.

4. INSURANCE

Since the property will be in your name, house flipping basics tells us you've got to cover it! It may be difficult to get homeowner's insurance for a wholesale property. Your best bet may be to pick up Builder's Risk Insurance. This is insurance that's intended for properties being built or in the process of being remodeled.

5. REPAIR COSTS

House Flippers will want to repair any damage to the cheap property they've just purchased. Naturally, you'll be responsible for remodeling costs and repair costs to the contractors you hire.

THE COSTS INVOLVED IN WHOLESALING

As soon as the average wholesaler gets a client to sign the agreement to sell their house, they should be out the door or on the phone looking for potential buyers. These buyers are usually other investors who like to buy houses cheaply and fix them up with their own house flipping costs. Buyers may even be hard money lenders who are looking to expand their business into new areas. These wholesaling costs can be very minimal. You'll be focused on selling that house before the agreement to sell the house reaches its closing date.

Wholesalers don't spend money to fix up the house, on insurance or even placing the property with a realtor if you can help it. You'll also usually be responsible for closing costs and even a referral bonus if someone referred the property lead to you.

1. APPRAISAL COSTS

Depending on where you are and how you close the deal, you may need to hire an appraiser to look over the house and give you an estimate of its market value.

2. HOME INSPECTION

Wholesaling property buyers aren't usually nervous about buying a home that needs some work, but they may want to know what kind of work needs to be done before purchase. Thus, you'll have to get a property inspector out there to evaluate the damage so you can present the information to your buyer.

3. LOAN COSTS OR CLOSING FEES

You may be responsible for one set of closing fees when you buy the house and sell it to your buyer. This depends on how you set up the sale. Most likely the title company will just deduct the closing costs from your profits before cutting you a check.

4. REFERRALS

Property wholesalers sometimes offer referral bonuses to people who provide them with property leads. This is usually about $500 to $1000.

5. ADVERTISING

You've got to get your name out there. Advertising doesn't need to cost much, just as much as a ream of paper and some printing ink or as much as a radio spot and classified ads in the local paper. This is up to you.

As you can see, house flipping costs are much higher than the process of wholesaling. Wholesaling costs can be very little for the investor, and involve wholesaling a lot of houses for an average of $3,000 to $5,000 profit. However, there are benefits of both options. House flipping costs a lot of money initially, but promises a bigger payoff on only one deal. Some flippers claim to make anywhere from $50,000 profit per sale all the way up to in rare cases of a whopping half a million dollars.

Check out "Flipping Houses: The Complete Guide on How to Buy, Sell and Invest in Real Estate" by K.

Connors to learn more!

Made in the USA
Monee, IL
19 November 2019